Heart Jewel

Also by Geshe Kelsang Gyatso

Meaningful to Behold
Clear Light of Bliss
Buddhism in the Tibetan Tradition
Heart of Wisdom
Universal Compassion
The Meditation Handbook
Joyful Path of Good Fortune
Guide to Dakini Land
The Bodhisattva Vow
Great Treasury of Merit
Introduction to Buddhism
Understanding the Mind
Tantric Grounds and Paths
Ocean of Nectar

Tharpa Publications is a publisher of Buddhist books that provide the most complete and integrated presentation of the Buddhist path to enlightenment available in any western language, from basic introductions to Buddhism and meditation to detailed and lucid expositions of the highest Buddhist philosophy and Tantric practice. There is a Tharpa website at http://www.luna.co.uk/~tharpa.

GESHE KELSANG GYATSO

Heart Jewel

THE ESSENTIAL PRACTICES
OF KADAMPA BUDDHISM

THARPA PUBLICATIONS
London

First published in 1991
Second edition reset 1997

The right of Geshe Kelsang Gyatso
to be identified as author of this work
has been asserted by him in accordance with
the Copyright, Designs, and Patents Act 1988.

Tharpa Publications
15 Bendemeer Road
London SW15 1JX

© Geshe Kelsang Gyatso and Manjushri Centre 1991, 1997

Cover painting of Je Tsongkhapa and his two Sons
descending from Tushita Pure Land by
the Tibetan artist Chating Jamyang Lama.
Cover design by Stefan Killen.
Cover photo of Geshe Kelsang Gyatso by Eric Martin.
Line illustrations by Andy Weber, Graham Dyer,
and Ani Kelsang Wangchen.

British Library Cataloguing in Publication Data
A catalogue record for this book is
available from the British Library.

ISBN 0 948006 55 2 – papercase
ISBN 0 948006 56 0 – paperback

Set in Palatino by Tharpa Publications.
Printed on acid-free 250-year longlife paper and bound
by Redwood Books, Trowbridge, Wiltshire, England.

Contents

Illustrations   vi
Acknowledgements   vii
Preface   viii

PART ONE: The Guru Yoga of Je Tsongkhapa
Introduction   3
Accumulating Merit   17
Receiving Attainments   31
The *Migtsema* Prayer   47
Close Retreat   53

PART TWO: Relying upon the Dharma Protector
Introduction to the Dharma Protector   71
Previous Incarnations of the Dharma Protector   75
The Nature and Function of the Dharma Protector   89
The Way to Rely upon the Dharma Protector   95
Dedication   98

Appendix I – The Condensed Meaning of the
   Commentary   99
Appendix II – The Dharma Protector's Mandala   105
Appendix III – Sadhanas
   Heart Jewel   111
   King of the Dharma   123
   Wishfulfilling Jewel   137
   Vajradaka Burning Offering   155

Glossary   161
Bibliography   174
Study Programmes   177
Index   178

Illustrations

Je Tsongkhapa and his two Sons descending from
    Tushita Pure Land   2
Je Sherab Senge   10
Palden Sangpo   18
Je Sangye Gyatso   24
Phabongkha Rinpoche   30
Trijang Rinpoche   38
Avalokiteshvara   46
Manjushri   54
Vajrapani   58
Je Tsongkhapa   64
The five lineages of Dorje Shugdän   70
The nine Great Mothers   74
The eight Fully Ordained Monks   88
The ten Wrathful Deities   96
The letter DHI   128

Acknowledgements

In the autumn of 1990 the students of Manjushri Mahayana Buddhist Centre had the great good fortune to receive from the precious and fully realized Master, Geshe Kelsang Gyatso, a complete series of clear and inspiring teachings on the Guru yoga of Je Tsongkhapa according to the Segyu lineage. These teachings have now been published as the present book.

In this book Geshe Kelsang establishes the authenticity and unique qualities of Je Tsongkhapa and the New Kadampa Tradition, thereby helping to promote this pure tradition throughout the world for succeeding generations. We thank the author most deeply for this inestimable kindness.

We would also like to thank all the students of the author who, with great skill and dedication, edited the book and prepared it for publication.

Roy Tyson,
Administrative Director,
Manjushri Mahayana
Buddhist Centre,
April 1997

Preface

This book presents two practices revealed by Manjushri, the Wisdom Buddha. The first is a special Guru yoga in which we visualize our Spiritual Guide as Je Tsongkhapa, who himself is an emanation of Buddha Manjushri. By relying upon this practice we can purify negativity, accumulate merit, and receive blessings. In this way we shall naturally accomplish all the realizations of the stages of the path of Sutra and Tantra, and in particular we shall attain a very special Dharma wisdom.

The second practice is a method for relying upon the Dharma Protector. Through this practice we can overcome obstacles to our practice and create favourable conditions so that we can nurture and increase our pure Dharma realizations.

These two practices are the essential practices of the New Kadampa Tradition of Mahayana Buddhism. They are both included in the sadhana *Heart Jewel*, which can be found in Appendix III. By practising this sadhana regularly and sincerely we shall make our precious human life extremely meaningful, and we shall definitely reap a harvest of pure Dharma realizations. Eventually we shall come to experience the supreme joy of full enlightenment.

PART ONE

------

*The Guru Yoga of
Je Tsongkhapa*

*Je Tsongkhapa and his two Sons descending
from Tushita Pure Land*

Introduction

The commentary to the sadhana *Heart Jewel* is given under three main headings:

  1 The instruction of the Guru yoga of Je Tsongkhapa according to the Segyu lineage
  2 Relying upon the Dharma Protector
  3 Dedication

The instruction of the Guru yoga of Je Tsongkhapa according to the Segyu lineage is presented in two parts:

  1 Introduction
  2 The actual practice of the instruction

The introduction has three parts:

  1 Je Tsongkhapa
  2 The history and lineage of the instruction
  3 The benefits of this practice

JE TSONGKHAPA

In *Root Tantra of Manjushri* Buddha Shakyamuni made a prediction about how Manjushri would later emanate as Je Tsongkhapa:

> After I pass away
> And my pure doctrine is absent,
> You will appear as an ordinary being,
> Performing the deeds of a Buddha
> And establishing the Joyful Land, the great Protector,
> In the Land of the Snows.

3

This verse reveals the special qualities of Je Tsongkhapa. The third line explains that although he was an enlightened being, a manifestation of the Wisdom Buddha Manjushri, Je Tsongkhapa did not reveal himself to be a special being but always appeared in the aspect of an ordinary practitioner. In particular he never made a public display of his miracle powers or clairvoyance, and he encouraged his disciples to follow his example by not revealing any special powers they might have attained.

Instead of revealing miracle powers Je Tsongkhapa mainly worked to establish pure Buddhadharma throughout Tibet. By giving teachings and showing a good example he led many beings to gain pure, authentic realizations of Sutra and Tantra. This is the meaning of the fourth line of the verse.

The phrase 'Joyful Land' in the fifth line is the name of Buddha Maitreya's Pure Land, known as 'Tushita' in Sanskrit or 'Ganden' in Tibetan, which is where Je Tsongkhapa went after he passed away. During his life Je Tsongkhapa established a great monastery in Tibet called 'Ganden Monastery', and he spread throughout Tibet a pure doctrine which became known as the 'Ganden doctrine'. This doctrine is a special, pure Buddhadharma that comes from Manjushri's wisdom. It is called 'the great Protector' because it protects all living beings from the ocean of samsaric suffering. All of this indicates that Je Tsongkhapa is a manifestation of Buddha Maitreya, who is the Protector of the hundreds of Deities of the Joyful Land. These days the tradition of Je Tsongkhapa is known as the 'Gelug', or 'Virtuous Tradition', and his followers are known as 'Gelugpas'; but the original name of 'Ganden' came from Buddha Shakyamuni. This is the meaning of the fifth line.

As Buddha had predicted, Je Tsongkhapa appeared in Tibet, the Land of the Snows, where he lived from 1357 to 1419. When he was born a drop of his mother's blood fell to the ground, and later a white sandal tree with a hundred thousand leaves grew at that spot. On each of the leaves there appeared an image of Buddha Sengei Ngaro, who is the same mental continuum as Buddha Manjushri. This indicates that the child was a manifestation of Manjushri. Later the third

Dalai Lama, Sönam Gyatso, said that this precious tree was an object of offerings and respect, and he moved it to a nearby monastery where he placed it inside a silver stupa with many precious jewels and made extensive offerings to it. This monastery became known as 'Kumbum Monastery', or 'The Monastery of a Hundred Thousand Images'. Eventually other similar trees grew around the stupa and their leaves also bore special images. On some there appeared the letters of Manjushri's mantra, AH RA PA TSA NA DHI, and on others the seed-letter of Manjushri, the letter DHI. These leaves were regarded as very precious, and when they fell in the autumn people would gather them and grind them into powder. Through tasting this powder many people have been able to cure diseases and increase their wisdom.

Je Tsongkhapa showed a perfect example of how to build the foundation for the spiritual path, how to progress on that path, and how to complete it. First he studied the entire Dharma of Sutra and Tantra by relying sincerely upon his Spiritual Guides, and then he put all this knowledge into practice and demonstrated the attainment of all the realizations from relying upon the Spiritual Guide up to the Union of No More Learning, or Buddhahood. Since then thousands of practitioners have attained the ultimate happiness of Buddhahood within one life by following Je Tsongkhapa's example and sincerely practising his teachings. Even today faithful practitioners who follow Je Tsongkhapa's pure Dharma can accomplish these results.

If instead of giving teachings and setting a pure example Je Tsongkhapa had mainly demonstrated his own good qualities by displaying miracle powers and other forms of clairvoyance, we would have received no benefit from his actions. What we need is not displays of miracle powers but a clear example of how to enter an unmistaken spiritual path, how to practise that path comfortably and smoothly, and how to complete it successfully. This is the actual method for solving our daily problems. Since Je Tsongkhapa provided us with just such an example, we should recognize his immense kindness and develop unchanging faith and respect for him.

Je Gendundrub, the first Dalai Lama, wrote a special praise to Je Tsongkhapa called *Song of the Eastern Snow Mountain*, or *Shargangrima* in Tibetan. In this song he says to Je Tsongkhapa:

For the fortunate people of Tibet, the Land of the Snows,
    your kindness, O Protector, is inconceivable.
Especially for myself, Gendundrub, an indolent one,
The fact that my mind is directed towards Dharma
Is due solely to your kindness, O Venerable Father
    and Sons.

From now until I attain enlightenment
I shall seek no refuge other than you.
O Venerable Father and Sons
Please care for me with your compassion.

Although I cannot repay your kindness, O Protector,
I pray that, with my mind free from the influence of
    attachment and hatred,
I may strive to maintain your doctrine and cause it
    to flourish
Without ever giving up this endeavour.

Just visualizing Je Tsongkhapa with faith is a powerful method for receiving the blessings of all the Buddhas, and, if we have strong faith, simply keeping a statue of Je Tsongkhapa in our house will cause that place to become a holy environment and will protect us from poverty.

When Je Tsongkhapa passed away, the whole country was overwhelmed with sorrow at the loss of their precious Teacher. Not only could they no longer see him directly but, since there were very few representations of him, most people were unable to see even his likeness. Consequently, many craftsmen set about making statues and painting tangkhas of him. Although Je Tsongkhapa had not publicly displayed his miracle powers while he was alive, after he passed away he performed many miracles through these statues and tangkhas. Eight statues in particular have since become very famous. They are known as:

(1) Je she par ma (The Venerable One who Disappeared with a Smile)

(2) Je nga dra ma (The Venerable One who is a Better Likeness)

(3) Je shen pän ma (The Venerable One who is More Beneficial to Others)

(4) Je ku thim ma (The Venerable One who Dissolved into the Body)

(5) Je nam pur ma (The Venerable One who Rose into Space)

(6) Je tsong pön gelek ma (The Venerable Chief Merchant Gelek)

(7) Je tsö dog ma (The Venerable One who Pacifies Conflicts)

(8) Je ling pur ma (The Venerable One Gone to Another Land)

The story of the first statue is as follows. At one time a humble practitioner tried to find a statue of Je Tsongkhapa for his retreat but was unsuccessful, so during his retreat he made a small statue and placed it on his shrine. For him this statue was like the living Je Tsongkhapa, and every day before beginning his meditation he made offerings and prostrations in front of it. One day as he rose from meditation he noticed that the statue was gradually melting into light. As he watched, the statue suddenly smiled and, rising into space, completely disappeared. The meditator was astonished and could hardly believe what he had seen. After reflecting for a long time he decided to go to his Teacher to tell him what had happened. His Teacher was delighted and told him to make another statue exactly like the previous one. This he did, and it is this statue that subsequently became known as 'The Venerable One who Disappeared with a Smile'.

The second and third statues were made by two craftsmen who were engaged in a friendly contest to see who was the more skilled at making statues. They took the two statues to a high Lama to adjudicate. As the Lama was examining them with a faithful mind, one statue spoke, saying 'I am a better likeness.' Then the other statue retorted 'But I am more beneficial to others.' This is how these two famous statues received their names.

The fourth statue is named after one that belonged to a practitioner called Nyungnä Lama, whose main practice was the Guru yoga of Je Tsongkhapa. He used to keep a statue of Je Tsongkhapa on his shrine, and he regarded this statue as the living Je Tsongkhapa. Each day he would practise Guru yoga from going for refuge up to dissolving Guru Tsongkhapa into his heart. Because he practised so sincerely he developed a very pure heart and attained a special experience of concentration. One day, while visualizing Je Tsongkhapa dissolving into his heart, he experienced his statue actually dissolving into him; and when he rose from meditation the statue on his shrine had completely disappeared. After this he quickly attained many high realizations. News of this event spread, and the craftsman who had made the statue became very famous. Later he made another statue of Je Tsongkhapa to which he gave the name, 'The Venerable One who Dissolved into the Body'.

The fifth statue belonged to a monastery where it was often seen by one particularly sincere practitioner to rise into space and then return to its place on the shrine. Because of this, the statue became known as 'The Venerable One who Rose into Space'.

The sixth statue was made by a government minister who was a faithful disciple of Je Tsongkhapa, and Je Tsongkhapa himself had blessed it. One day, however, an evil person out of jealousy stole the statue and, taking it a long way away, threw it into a large river. Some time later an important merchant called Gelek was travelling on horseback in that area when he noticed a brightly-coloured rainbow standing vertically in space, apparently emerging from the bed of a river. Thinking that this was an unusual sign, he decided to spend the night nearby. The next morning the rainbow was still there and so he decided to investigate further. Although the local people could see nothing in the river, Gelek was not convinced. Securing himself with ropes he waded into the icy river and dived to the bottom. There he found the statue of Je Tsongkhapa radiating brightly-coloured rainbow lights. When he came to the surface the onlookers were astonished to see that he had not drowned, and even more astonished to see the precious statue that he was holding. Since it was the chief merchant Gelek who retrieved the statue, it subsequently became known as 'The Venerable Chief Merchant Gelek'.

The seventh statue comes from a part of eastern Tibet where at one time there was prolonged civil war. The local people longed for the fighting to stop, and so they went to a nearby Lama who was renowned as a great meditator and asked him what they should do. He told them to construct a large statue of Je Tsongkhapa in their town and make offerings and requests in front of it. This they did, and soon afterwards the fighting stopped and peace prevailed throughout the region. This statue later became known as 'The Venerable One who Pacifies Conflicts'.

The eighth statue is named after a much revered statue of Je Tsongkhapa that mysteriously disappeared from Tibet. Pure practitioners with clairvoyance realized that the statue had gone to another land far away where the ground was strewn with diamonds and where the language and customs were completely different. They also realized that the statue was benefiting the people of that land, and so they decided to make another one similar to it and named it 'The Venerable One Gone to Another Land'.

Miracles such as these are not confined to ancient times. Even today there are many statues and other representations of Je Tsongkhapa that possess special qualities. For example, there was one Geshe called Geshe Jatse whom I knew well when I was at Sera Monastery in Tibet. When he had completed his Geshe training he withdrew to a mountain cave to do retreat and remained there, living just like Milarepa, for the rest of his life. When he died, his many disciples, together with a large number of onlookers, went to the cave to pay their respects, and to their astonishment saw that Geshe Jatse's statue of Je Tsongkhapa had grown teeth and hair. I heard

Je Sherab Senge

this account directly from these disciples, some of whom I knew well.

My first Teacher in philosophy at Ngamring Jampaling Monastery was called Geshe Palden. At one time he did a long close retreat on Je Tsongkhapa counting *Migtsema* prayers. At the end of his retreat an image of Je Tsongkhapa appeared on one of the beads of his mala. He showed this to me and I saw it very clearly.

There are many other stories such as these which show that even in these impure times faithful practitioners can receive unceasing blessings from Je Tsongkhapa.

THE HISTORY AND LINEAGE OF THE INSTRUCTION

The Guru yoga of Je Tsongkhapa according to the Segyu lineage was originally taught by Buddha Manjushri as part of a special scripture known as the *Kadam Emanation Scripture*. It was extracted from this scripture by Je Tsongkhapa himself. These days the practice is known as *Ganden Lhagyäma* in Tibetan, or *The Hundreds of Deities of the Joyful Land* in English. The name derives from the fact that in the first verse we invite Je Tsongkhapa to descend from the heart of Buddha Maitreya, who is known as the 'Protector of the hundreds of Deities of the Joyful Land'.

Je Tsongkhapa passed this instruction to Je Sherab Senge, who was one of his main disciples. Je Sherab Senge was born in the upper part of Tibet called Tsang. He was a very holy meditation master and scholar who had thousands of disciples, including Je Gendundrub, the first Dalai Lama. He was the holder of the lineage of the Tantric teachings of Je Tsongkhapa and, as predicted by Je Tsongkhapa, he established Gyumä Tantric College in central Tibet and Segyu Tantric College in the upper part of Tibet.

Je Sherab Senge passed this instruction to Dulnagpa Palden Sangpo, who was one of his main disciples. Palden Sangpo was also born in Tsang, in a town called Tanagdo near Tashilhunpo Monastery, and he was ordained at Narthang Monastery. After receiving this instruction he practised it sincerely and as a result gained very high spiritual realizations. He was able to help many sick people by curing serious diseases and by pacifying obstacles through healing actions performed in conjunction with the *Migtsema* prayer.

In general, there are many people who are harmed by spirits called 'Behar'. These spirits enter into people's bodies causing them to become insane, interfering with their spiritual development, or causing untimely death. Once, while Palden Sangpo was engaged in a retreat on the *Migtsema* prayer at a place called Säpu, a Behar spirit began to harm a rich family who lived nearby. Many of their relatives had already been killed by such spirits, and now this spirit was trying to enter into the body of the son of the family. The members of the family were very worried and they requested Palden Sangpo to stop the spirit harming their son. Palden Sangpo accepted their request and gave the father a number of beads from the mala he had used during his *Migtsema* recitation. He told him, 'When the spirit enters your son's body, immediately place one bead at every exit to your house. This may cause the spirit to cry out in terror, and if this happens, call me.' The father did exactly as Palden Sangpo had said, and in this way trapped the spirit in his house. The spirit was terrified and cried, 'I want to escape from this house but many powerful and terrifying wrathful beings are preventing me.'

The father immediately went to Palden Sangpo and requested him to come to his house. When Palden Sangpo arrived he asked the spirit, 'How can you inflict harm on many mother sentient beings when you yourself cannot bear even this slight suffering? From now on you must not harm anyone else. If you do not promise to stop harming others, Yamantaka will not let you go.' The spirit replied, 'I follow the orders of the chief Behar spirit. If I do not harm anyone my powers will diminish and I shall suffer. Please do not ask so much of me, please reduce the commitment.' Palden Sangpo told the spirit, 'At least you must promise me that you will not harm anyone who recites the *Ganden Lhagyäma* or *Migtsema* prayers', and the spirit said, 'Yes, I can promise you this.' Palden Sangpo then gathered up the beads of his mala from the exits to the house and the spirit immediately left the boy's body and fled. The boy became normal again and did not suffer further. Later, people clearly realized that anyone who recites the *Ganden Lhagyäma* and *Migtsema* prayers will be protected from harm by Behar spirits.

Both the *Ganden Lhagyäma* and the *Migtsema* prayers come from the *Kadam Emanation Scripture*. This scripture, which is the same nature as Manjushri's wisdom, cannot be seen by ordinary beings, and the instructions it contains are not written in ordinary letters. So that ordinary beings could see these prayers, Palden Sangpo wrote them out in ordinary letters, in the form of prose. Later, Khädrub Sangye Gyatso wrote the verses that we now recite.

Je Palden Sangpo passed this instruction on to Gyuchen Gendunpai, who passed it on to Gyuchen Tashipa, who passed it on to Je Samdrub Gyatso, who passed it on to Tsöndrupa, who passed it on to Dorje Sangpo, who passed it on to Khädrub Sangye Gyatso. Eventually the instruction reached Je Phabongkhapa and Kyabje Trijang Dorjechang, spiritual Father and Son.

This lineage is an uncommon close lineage that comes from Buddha Shakyamuni to Manjushri, and directly from Manjushri to Je Tsongkhapa, Je Sherab Senge, and so on. Through the kindness of Je Sherab Senge, Je Palden Sangpo, and Khädrub Sangye Gyatso, this instruction flourished throughout Tibet. Since these Lamas came from the area called Se, in the region of Tashilhunpo Monastery, the lineage is called the 'Segyu lineage'.

THE BENEFITS OF THIS PRACTICE

When we practise the Guru yoga of Je Tsongkhapa according to the Segyu lineage we meditate on our root Guru in the aspect of Je Tsongkhapa – the embodiment of Avalokiteshvara, Manjushri, and Vajrapani, offer the seven limbs and the mandala offering, make requests with the *Migtsema* prayer, and then engage in the stages of the practice of profound meditations.

Through practising sincerely in this way we can pacify all our negative karma and obstacles and increase our merit, life span, and Dharma realizations. In particular, because Je Tsongkhapa is at once an emanation of Avalokiteshvara (the embodiment of all Buddhas' compassion), Manjushri (the embodiment of all Buddhas' wisdom), and Vajrapani (the embodiment of all Buddhas' power), we can easily increase our realizations of compassion, wisdom, and spiritual power. Of these it is especially important to increase our wisdom because wisdom is the antidote to ignorance, the root of all our suffering. As Buddha says in the *Perfection of Wisdom Sutra*, those who lack wisdom are like blind people who continually experience problems and suffering because they cannot see. The best method for increasing our wisdom, and thereby protecting ourself from suffering, is to practise the Guru yoga of Je Tsongkhapa, because Je Tsongkhapa is a manifestation of the wisdom of all the Buddhas.

On the basis of pacifying our negativity and obstacles and increasing our life span, merit, compassion, wisdom, and spiritual power, if we rely upon this practice we shall easily gain all the realizations of Sutra and Tantra and eventually attain the Union of No More Learning, or Buddhahood. Because followers of Je Tsongkhapa have a special connection with him, all these beneficial results of entering into Je Tsongkhapa's doctrine can be achieved with great ease by practising this Guru yoga.

As we have seen, Palden Sangpo controlled Behar spirits, protected many people from untimely death, and pacified their suffering through the practice of reciting the *Ganden Lhagyäma* and *Migtsema* prayers. In the account mentioned above, the Behar spirit saw the beads of Palden Sangpo's mala as terrifying wrathful beings, who in reality were Yamantaka. This clearly indicates that accomplishing the attainment of Je Tsongkhapa has the same function as accomplishing the attainment of Yamantaka, reciting the *Migtsema* prayer has the same function as reciting the mantra of Yamantaka, meditating on Je Tsongkhapa has the same function as meditating on Yamantaka, and so on. 'Yamantaka', or 'Shin je she' in

Tibetan, means 'opponent of outer, inner, and secret obstacles'. Thus, the practices of *Ganden Lhagyäma* and *Migtsema* are powerful methods for pacifying these three types of obstacle. Outer obstacles include harm from humans or non-humans, dangers from the outer elements such as fire and water, different kinds of accident, and lacking the necessary conditions for spiritual practice. Inner obstacles include sickness, strong delusions, and negative thoughts that arise within our mind. Secret obstacles are ordinary appearances, ordinary conceptions, and subtle dualistic appearance.

Although both Yamantaka and Je Tsongkhapa are manifestations of Manjushri, for followers of Je Tsongkhapa the practices of *Ganden Lhagyäma* and *Migtsema* are more powerful than the practice of Yamantaka. There are three reasons for this: (1) followers of Je Tsongkhapa have a direct connection with Je Tsongkhapa's doctrine; (2) the practices of *Ganden Lhagyäma* and *Migtsema* were taught directly by Manjushri himself, and Je Tsongkhapa is the principal Guru of this practice; and (3) the instruction of *Ganden Lhagyäma* and *Migtsema* has the uncommon close lineage mentioned above. When we accomplish the practice of *Ganden Lhagyäma* and *Migtsema*, we accomplish not only the practices of wrathful and peaceful Manjushri, but also the practices of Avalokiteshvara and Vajrapani.

Mahasiddha Menkhangpa said, 'The unmistaken Dharma is Lamrim, Lojong, and Mahamudra.' Here, 'Mahamudra' refers to Vajrayana Mahamudra, which contains the practices of both generation stage and completion stage of Secret Mantra. The instruction on these three Dharmas – Lamrim (the stages of the path), Lojong (training the mind), and Mahamudra – is the heart of Je Tsongkhapa's doctrine and the very essence of Buddhadharma. To gain the realizations of these three Dharmas we must receive into our mind the powerful blessings of Je Tsongkhapa by sincerely engaging in the practice of the *Ganden Lhagyäma* and *Migtsema* prayers.

Mahasiddha Menkhangpa and the Panchen Lama, Palden Yeshe, composed eleven different instructions on ritual healing practices in conjunction with the *Migtsema* prayer. These are practices: (1) to make rain for crops, (2) to gather clouds, (3) to cure the 'drib' disease, a physical disease caused by spirits that makes people fall and become unconscious without any visible reasons, (4) to avoid harm from weapons, (5) to prevent future drib diseases, (6) to cure wind, or 'lung', diseases, (7) to cure physical and mental disabilities, (8) to protect against thieves, robbers, and enemies, (9) to pacify obstacles to growing crops, such as insects, (10) to find food, and (11) to pacify obstacles when travelling. Those who have completed an action close retreat of *Migtsema* can perform these healing practices to benefit others.

Altogether there are one hundred and eight ritual practices in conjunction with the *Migtsema* prayer that have been written by different authors. They are all methods for helping sentient beings.

The practice of *Migtsema* is very important for fulfilling both one's own and others' wishes. Through not understanding the benefits of reciting the *Migtsema* prayer many people disregard this practice. Others ignore it, thinking that it is just a small practice. Some even think 'This practice is small, whereas I am a great practitioner.' Such an attitude is a wrong conception. Once a Mongolian minister asked the Panchen Lama, Palden Yeshe, to give him a small practice that he could do every day because he was otherwise very busy. The Panchen Lama asked him what kind of practice he wanted and the Mongolian replied that he would like to receive the instruction on the *Migtsema* practice. The Panchen Lama was surprised, and said, 'How can you say that the practice of *Migtsema* is a small practice? There is no greater practice than this; it contains the meaning of all Buddha's eighty-four thousand teachings!'

Accumulating Merit

THE ACTUAL PRACTICE OF THE INSTRUCTION

The actual practice of the instruction of the Guru yoga of Je Tsongkhapa according to the Segyu lineage has three parts:

1 The actual practice
2 An explanation of the Migtsema prayer
3 How to do a close retreat of Migtsema

The actual practice has two parts:

1 The practice during the meditation session
2 The practice during the meditation break

The practice during the meditation session has five parts:

1 The preliminary practices of going for refuge and generating bodhichitta
2 Inviting the Field for Accumulating Merit
3 Accumulating merit
4 Receiving attainments by making requests
5 Conclusion

THE PRELIMINARY PRACTICES OF GOING FOR REFUGE AND GENERATING BODHICHITTA

This has four parts:

1 The objects of refuge
2 Generating the causes of going for refuge
3 The prayer of going for refuge
4 Generating bodhichitta

Palden Sangpo

THE OBJECTS OF REFUGE

We visualize the objects of refuge by contemplating as follows:

In the space before me is the living Buddha Shakyamuni surrounded by all the Buddhas and Bodhisattvas, like the full moon surrounded by stars.

GENERATING THE CAUSES OF GOING FOR REFUGE

We generate the causes of going for refuge by contemplating as follows:

I and all my kind mothers, fearing samsara's torments, turn to Buddha, Dharma, and Sangha, the only sources of refuge. From now until enlightenment, to the Three Jewels we go for refuge.

THE PRAYER OF GOING FOR REFUGE

Having generated the causes of refuge, we now go for refuge while reciting the following prayer three times:

I and all sentient beings, until we achieve enlightenment, Go for refuge to Buddha, Dharma, and Sangha.

GENERATING BODHICHITTA

We then generate a motivation of bodhichitta while reciting the following prayer three times:

Through the virtues I collect by giving and other perfections, May I become a Buddha for the benefit of all.

INVITING THE FIELD FOR ACCUMULATING MERIT

The principal beings in the Field for Accumulating Merit in this practice are Je Tsongkhapa and his two main disciples, Gyaltsabje and Khädrubje. Je Tsongkhapa is a manifestation of Manjushri, the nature of all Buddhas' wisdom; Gyaltsabje a manifestation of Avalokiteshvara, the nature of all Buddhas' compassion; and Khädrubje a manifestation of Vajrapani, the nature of all Buddhas' power.

We invite Je Tsongkhapa and his two spiritual Sons to come from Joyful Land, Tushita, to the space before us. As mentioned before, Je Tsongkhapa went to Tushita after he passed away and so we begin by visualizing him together with his two Sons at the heart of Buddha Maitreya within this Pure Land. This reminds us that Je Tsongkhapa and Buddha Maitreya are the same mental continuum.

Many great Teachers went to Tushita Pure Land after they passed away. Atisha, for example, told his faithful disciples, 'In my next life I shall go to Joyful Land. Those who have faith in me will meet me there.' Accordingly, after he passed away Atisha went to Tushita Pure Land where he appeared as a principal disciple of Maitreya called 'Stainless Space' (Tib. Namkha Drime). He gave Dharma teachings to his disciples in Tushita and sent many emanations to this world. Some time later Atisha's main disciple, Dromtönpa, established Reting Monastery, and during the puja for blessing the monastery, known in Tibetan as the 'rabnä puja', he requested Stainless Space to bless the monastery. Stainless Space did so by throwing flowers from Tushita onto the roof of the monastery. Later many practitioners of the Old Kadampa Tradition, including Dromtönpa himself, chose to be reborn in Tushita so as to be close to their Spiritual Guide.

Just like Atisha, Je Tsongkhapa also went to Tushita Pure Land, where he appeared as a main Bodhisattva disciple of Maitreya called 'Essence of Manjushri' (Tib. Jampel Nyingpo). He gave many teachings to his disciples in Tushita and sent countless emanations to this world. Just as many practitioners of the Old Kadampa Tradition chose to be reborn in Tushita to be close to their Spiritual Guide, Atisha, so many practitioners of the New Kadampa Tradition, including Khädrubje and Gyaltsabje, chose to be reborn in this Pure Land so as to be close to Je Tsongkhapa.

To gain a rough image of what Tushita Pure Land is like, we can contemplate the following description:

To the north of this continent, Jambudipa, is Mount Meru, which has four stepped levels. On top of Mount Meru is Land of the Thirty-three Heavens, the second abode of the desire realm gods; in the space above this is Land Without Combat, the third abode of the desire realm gods; and in the space above this is Joyful Land, the fourth abode of the desire realm gods. Just above this god realm is the Pure Land of Buddha Maitreya, which is also known as Joyful Land, or Tushita. Beings who abide in Tushita Pure Land do not experience ageing, sickness, or any other suffering, and they acquire whatever they need effortlessly. In this place there is not even the sound of poverty or fighting, and no danger from fire, water, wind, or earth. The environment is completely pure, clean, and very beautiful, and there are many objects of enjoyment such as precious mountains, wishfulfilling trees, beautiful lakes, and pools. In the trees many delightful birds, which are emanations of Maitreya, make sounds that reveal the meaning of Dharma. There are also many beautiful gardens filled with exquisite jewels, heavenly flowers, and precious bathing pools in which fortunate young gods and goddesses play. The whole ground is made of jewels and is completely pure and smooth. Just touching it gives rise to bliss. In the centre of this Pure Land is the Yiga Chödzin Palace where Buddha Maitreya lives with a retinue of thousands of Bodhisattvas.

To invite Je Tsongkhapa Father and Sons to the space before us we begin by visualizing them at the heart of Buddha Maitreya, indicating that they will come from Maitreya's Truth Body, the space of the Dharmakaya:

In the Yiga Chödzin Palace, on a jewelled throne supported by eight snow lions, sits Buddha Maitreya, who has a golden-coloured body. His two hands at the level of his heart in the gesture of turning the Wheel of Dharma hold flowers from a naga tree. These support a wheel and a long-necked vase. He is seated on a throne with his feet on the ground, indicating his readiness to descend from Tushita to this world. At his heart is Je Tsongkhapa, with Gyaltsabje to his right and Khädrubje to his left. They sit on a cluster of clouds which resemble a mass of fresh, white curd, and which are a manifestation of Maitreya's compassion. They each wear the saffron robes of an ordained person.

Having visualized this clearly we recite the verse from the sadhana inviting Je Tsongkhapa and his two Sons, together with all the Buddhas and Bodhisattvas, to come to the space in front of us as objects for accumulating merit. We strongly imagine that due to our invitation prayer Je Tsongkhapa Father and Sons come from the clouds of compassion at Maitreya's heart to the space before us:

> *White clouds billow from Maitreya's heart and descend to the space in front of us, just like a ball of wool unravelling with one end of the thread remaining connected to Maitreya's heart. At the same time Je Tsongkhapa and his two Sons descend and sit on thrones on the clouds.*

This way of inviting Je Tsongkhapa and his Sons is very special because it indicates that, from the space of Maitreya's Truth Body, clouds of his compassion for the beings of this world arise, and as a result a rain of Dharma teachings continually descends upon the beings of this world through Je Tsongkhapa and his emanations.

At this point we visualize as follows:

> *In the space in front of us there are three jewelled thrones with the central throne slightly higher than the other two. Each throne is supported by eight snow lions. On the central throne, on a lotus, moon, and sun cushion, sits our root Guru in the aspect of Je Tsongkhapa, who is the embodiment of Manjushri, Avalokiteshvara, and Vajrapani; on the throne to his right, on a lotus, moon, and sun cushion, sits Gyaltsabje, who is a manifestation of Avalokiteshvara; and on the throne to his left, on a lotus, moon, and sun cushion, sits Khädrubje, who is a manifestation of Vajrapani.*
>
> *Their bodies are made of wisdom light, and are white with a reddish tint. They wear the three robes of an ordained person, signifying that they have completed the perfection of the three moral disciplines; and yellow long-eared hats, signifying that they have completed the perfection of wisdom. They are sitting on jewelled thrones which are supported by eight lions, symbolizing their four fearlessnesses in general, and their four protections that protect sentient beings from the*

four maras in particular. The lotus, moon, and sun cushions signify their complete purity of body and mind, their conventional bodhichitta, and their ultimate bodhichitta respectively. Their sitting in the vajra posture indicates that they have attained the Union of No More Learning.

Je Tsongkhapa's two hands at the level of his heart, in the gesture of turning the Wheel of Dharma, indicate that he can dispel the ignorance of sentient beings by giving teachings. He holds stems of upala flowers, which support a wisdom sword and a scripture of the Perfection of Wisdom Sutra in Eight Thousand Lines. *These signify that he principally teaches the profound Madhyamika-Prasangika view explained in the* Perfection of Wisdom Sutras *(symbolized by the scripture) by means of his omniscient wisdom (symbolized by the sword), motivated by love and compassion (symbolized by the two flowers). The right hands of the two Sons are at the level of their hearts in the gesture of expounding Dharma, and their left hands are in the gesture of meditative equipoise holding scriptures, signifying that Je Tsongkhapa's doctrine will spread throughout the world.*

At the centre of Je Tsongkhapa's crown chakra on a lotus and moon cushion is Manjushri, with an orange-coloured body, one face, and two arms; at the centre of his throat chakra on a lotus and moon cushion is Avalokiteshvara, with a white-coloured body, one face, and four arms; and at the centre of his heart chakra on a lotus and sun cushion is Vajrapani, with a blue-coloured body, one face, and two arms. They are all complete with their usual features such as ornaments, clothes, gestures, and implements. Je Tsongkhapa and his two Sons are surrounded by all the Buddhas and Bodhisattvas.

Visualizing in this way we should strongly believe that Je Tsongkhapa and all the other holy beings are actually present in the space before us, and generate a mind of deep faith.

Since Maitreya is an enlightened being he is the Protector of all sentient beings, but in the sadhana it says that Maitreya is the 'Protector of the hundreds of Deities of the Joyful Land'. This indicates that the hundreds of millions of fortunate beings who abide in Tushita Pure Land have a special

Je Sangye Gyatso

opportunity to receive teachings directly from Maitreya. The words 'King of the Dharma' signify that Je Tsongkhapa is like the crown ornament of all the Dharma Teachers in Tibet, and that his Dharma teachings are the king of all teachings.

ACCUMULATING MERIT

We now offer the practice of the seven limbs to Je Tsong-khapa and all the other holy beings so as to accumulate a vast collection of merit that will enable us to fulfil all our spiritual hopes and wishes. For auspiciousness we begin with the limb of requesting the Spiritual Guide to remain for a long time, which is normally recited as the fifth limb.

REQUESTING THE SPIRITUAL GUIDE TO REMAIN FOR A LONG TIME

If the Spiritual Guides who lead sentient beings on spiritual paths were no longer to appear in this world, the people of this world would have no opportunity to go for refuge or to accumulate merit, and there would be no possibility of their escaping from the sufferings of samsara and gaining pure happiness. From a spiritual point of view the world would be plunged into darkness. So as to prevent this happening we now request the holy beings, the Buddhas, to remain for countless aeons as emanations who will lead sentient beings on the spiritual path. This practice is a very powerful method for accumulating merit, and is extremely important for the future happiness of sentient beings.

We strongly believe that Je Tsongkhapa in the space before us is in essence our Spiritual Guide and we imagine that he is smiling at us with delight, just like a mother delighted with her dearest child. We visualize Je Tsongkhapa surrounded by all the Gurus, Yidams, Buddhas, and Bodhisattvas, and by reciting the prayer from the sadhana request them from the depths of our heart to remain with samsaric beings until samsara has ceased. We request them to remain as our supreme Field for Accumulating Merit so that we may sow the seeds of faith, cultivate the crops of the collections of merit and wisdom, and enjoy the ultimate harvest of full enlightenment.

PROSTRATION

Prostrations are a powerful method for purifying negative karma, sickness, and obstacles, and for increasing our merit, our happiness, and our Dharma realizations. Temporarily prostrations improve our physical health, and ultimately they cause us to attain a Buddha's Form Body. Generating faith in the holy beings is mental prostration, reciting praises to them is verbal prostration, and showing respect to them with our body is physical prostration. We can make physical prostrations by respectfully prostrating our entire body on the ground; by respectfully touching our knees, palms, and forehead to the ground; or by respectfully placing our palms together at the level of our heart.

To make special prostrations to Je Tsongkhapa we begin by contemplating the pre-eminent qualities of his mind, his speech, and his body. Since Je Tsongkhapa has abandoned the obstructions to omniscience his mind knows all phenomena without exception, and he realizes all conventional truths and all ultimate truths clearly, directly, and simultaneously. Simply hearing Je Tsongkhapa's speech causes fortunate beings to experience pure happiness, so for them his speech is a supreme ear ornament that gives rise to uncontaminated bliss. Je Tsongkhapa's body is extremely pleasing to behold because it is adorned with all the major signs and minor indications of a Buddha's Form Body. Thus, just by seeing Je Tsongkhapa's actual body or image, hearing his actual speech or his teachings, or remembering his good qualities, we accumulate a vast collection of merit and wisdom. Remembering this we generate deep faith in Je Tsongkhapa and then, in order to make powerful prostrations to him, we imagine that from every pore of our body we emanate another body, and from every pore of these bodies we emanate yet more bodies, until our emanated bodies fill the entire world. Then while reciting the verse from the sadhana we strongly believe that all these countless bodies make prostrations to Je Tsongkhapa, the principal Field for Accumulating Merit, and to all the other Gurus, Yidams, Buddhas, Bodhisattvas, Dakas, Dakinis, and Dharma Protectors.

OFFERINGS

We imagine that all the oceans, lakes, pools, springs, and rivers in the world transform into nectar for drinking, pure bathing water, and perfume. We think that these pure waters, together with all the flowers, incense, light, food, and music in the world, have the nature of exalted wisdom and function to cause the holy beings to experience uncontaminated bliss. Then we offer all these substances, each in their own aspect such as nectar for drinking, bathing water, and so forth, to the holy Gurus – Je Tsongkhapa and his retinue – while reciting the verse from the sadhana.

PURIFICATION

Since beginningless time we have created many negativities through our bodily, verbal, and mental actions. If these actions ripen on us they will result in our taking countless rebirths as hell beings, hungry ghosts, and animals. Moreover, many times in our previous lives we broke our spiritual commitments and the three sets of vows – the Pratimoksha vows, the Bodhisattva vows, and the Tantric vows. The result of these transgressions will be that our spiritual progress will be retarded and we shall find it more difficult to gain realizations. Realizing this, we generate deep regret and decide very strongly not to repeat such actions in the future. With this thought we purify our negativities by confessing them to the holy beings with the verse from the sadhana.

REJOICING

In his autobiography Je Tsongkhapa says that first he studied Dharma extensively, then he realized that all of Buddha's teachings are personal advice, and finally he gained deep realizations of Dharma through practising day and night. He then dedicated all his activities to the flourishing of pure Buddhadharma. In short, in this degenerate age Je Tsongkhapa showed the best example for Dharma practitioners to follow. He taught what pure Buddhadharma is, how to study and practise Dharma, and how to accomplish complete realizations. Contemplating this, we rejoice from the depths of our heart in his great deeds while reciting the verse from the sadhana.

REQUESTING THE TURNING OF THE WHEEL OF DHARMA

Buddha Shakyamuni demonstrated the manner of attaining the great liberation of full enlightenment at Bodh Gaya, but if he had not subsequently taught the Dharma that he experienced, the people of this world would have had no chance to attain liberation from the ocean of samsaric suffering. Therefore, while Buddha was in meditative equipoise the gods Brahma and Indra made the following request to him:

Without a Protector to provide protection
The blind migrators of this world will fall into the
    lower realms;
O Treasure of Compassion, please rise from your
    meditation
And turn the Wheel of Dharma.

As a result of Brahma and Indra making this request, Buddha gave many Dharma teachings that are the medicine for curing the diseases of delusions. From that time until now countless beings have attained complete liberation from samsaric suffering through sincerely practising Buddha's teachings. In a similar way, although there are many emanations of Je Tsongkhapa in the world, if they do not teach Je Tsongkhapa's Dharma the people of this world will have no chance to hear this special Dharma, put it into practice, and gain pure realizations. Therefore, by reciting the verse from the sadhana we make a special request for the turning of the Wheel of Dharma.

DEDICATION

There is a prayer that says:

By my riding the horse of virtue,
Directing it along correct paths with the reins of
    dedication,

And urging it with the whip of joyous effort,
May all beings reach the city of great liberation.

Since the attainment of great liberation depends upon pure Buddhadharma flourishing, we dedicate all our virtues to this end and pray that all sentient beings will thereby attain great enlightenment. We recite the verse from the sadhana.

OFFERING THE MANDALA

The word 'mandala' in this context means 'universe'. When we offer a mandala to the holy beings we are offering every- thing – the whole universe with all its objects and all the beings who inhabit it. Since the merit we create when we make an offering accords with the nature of the offering, we mentally transform the whole universe into a Pure Land and imagine that all its objects are precious substances. We then imagine that we are offering this pure universe in our hands.

A child once filled a bowl with dust and, imagining that the dust was gold, offered it to Buddha Kashyapa. As a result of this pure offering the child was reborn as the wealthy King Ashoka. Likewise, if we offer the world as a Pure Land filled with exquisite objects and precious symbols we shall experi- ence special, pure results. If we wish to experience happiness in the future, and especially if we wish for spiritual attain- ments, we should offer a mandala every day. For more infor- mation on the practice of the seven limbs and the mandala offering see *Joyful Path of Good Fortune*.

Phabongkha Rinpoche

Receiving Attainments

Receiving attainments by making requests has two parts:

1 Making requests
2 Receiving attainments

MAKING REQUESTS

In this context there are three ways of making requests:

1 Making requests with regard to Je Tsongkhapa's outer qualities
2 Making requests with regard to Je Tsongkhapa's inner qualities
3 Making requests with regard to Je Tsongkhapa's secret qualities

MAKING REQUESTS WITH REGARD TO JE TSONGKHAPA'S OUTER QUALITIES

With regard to the qualities of scriptural knowledge and the skilful means to teach others, Avalokiteshvara, Manjushri, and Vajrapani are unequalled among all the Bodhisattvas. In a similar way, with regard to these same qualities, Je Tsong-khapa, or Losang Dragpa, is unequalled among all the scholars of Tibet. Knowing this, with deep faith we make requests by reciting the following *Migtsema* prayer:

Tsongkhapa, crown ornament of the scholars of the Land of the Snows,
You are Avalokiteshvara, the treasury of unobservable compassion,
Manjushri, the supreme stainless wisdom,
And Vajrapani, the destroyer of the host of maras;

O Losang Dragpa I request you, please grant your
blessings.
You have knowledge of all the scriptures;
Please bless me to become just like you.

MAKING REQUESTS WITH REGARD TO JE TSONGKHAPA'S INNER QUALITIES

With regard to their inner realizations, Avalokiteshvara, Manjushri, and Vajrapani are unequalled among all the Bodhisattvas; and in a similar way, since he too possesses all these realizations, Je Tsongkhapa is unequalled among all the scholars of Tibet. Knowing this, with deep faith we make requests by reciting the following *Migtsema* prayer:

Tsongkhapa, crown ornament of the scholars of the Land
of the Snows,
You are Avalokiteshvara, the treasury of unobservable
compassion,
Manjushri, the supreme stainless wisdom,
And Vajrapani, the destroyer of the host of maras;
O Losang Dragpa I request you, please grant your
blessings.
You have accomplished all the realizations;
Please bless me to become just like you.

MAKING REQUESTS WITH REGARD TO JE TSONGKHAPA'S SECRET QUALITIES

Manjushri is the essence of the wisdom of all the Buddhas, Avalokiteshvara is the essence of the compassion of all the Buddhas, Vajrapani is the essence of the spiritual power of all the Buddhas; and Je Tsongkhapa is the synthesis of these three holy beings. Knowing this, with deep faith we make requests by reciting the following *Migtsema* prayer:

Tsongkhapa, crown ornament of the scholars of the Land
of the Snows,
You are Avalokiteshvara, the treasury of unobservable
compassion,

Manjushri, the supreme stainless wisdom,
And Vajrapani, the destroyer of the host of maras;
O Losang Dragpa I request you, please grant your
blessings.
You are the synthesis of all these holy beings;
Please bless me to become just like you.

When we are emphasizing the study of Dharma scriptures we recite principally the first version of the *Migtsema* prayer; when we are emphasizing gaining realizations by engaging in actual practices we recite principally the second version; and when we are emphasizing the practice of Secret Mantra we recite principally the third version.

RECEIVING ATTAINMENTS

This has two parts:

1 Purifying impurities
2 Accomplishing wisdom and attaining the
  realizations of the stages of the path

PURIFYING IMPURITIES

While reciting the *Migtsema* prayer and concentrating on its meaning, we sincerely request Je Tsongkhapa and his two Sons to dispel the inner darkness of our ignorance and other delusions and to purify all our negative karma and obstacles. Then we imagine that from the hearts of the Venerable Father and Sons there radiate white rays of light, which are hollow like straws. At our crown the tips of all three rays of light merge together to become one. We then strongly imagine that from the hearts of Je Tsongkhapa and his two Sons white wisdom-nectar, in the aspect of milk, flows through the rays of light and enters our body through our crown. Our body fills with light and wisdom-nectar, which purifies our ignorance and all our other delusions, as well as all our negative karma and obstacles. Our entire body becomes the nature of wisdom-light. We meditate on this feeling single-pointedly for as long as possible.

ACCOMPLISHING WISDOM AND ATTAINING THE REALIZATIONS OF THE STAGES OF THE PATH

This has two parts:

1 Accomplishing wisdom
2 Attaining the realizations of the stages of the path

ACCOMPLISHING WISDOM

This has two parts:

1 An introduction to the seven types of wisdom
2 The actual practice

AN INTRODUCTION TO THE SEVEN TYPES OF WISDOM

We can accomplish seven types of wisdom:

1 Great wisdom
2 Clear wisdom
3 Quick wisdom
4 Profound wisdom
5 The wisdom of expounding Dharma
6 The wisdom of spiritual debate
7 The wisdom of composing Dharma books

GREAT WISDOM

If we can understand easily, perfectly, and without difficulty all the objects that we need to abandon, such as true sufferings and true origins, and all the objects that we need to accomplish, such as true cessations and true paths, this indicates that we have great wisdom.

CLEAR WISDOM

If we can clearly distinguish the subtle characteristics of phenomena, such as the sixteen characteristics of the four noble truths, this indicates that we have clear wisdom.

QUICK WISDOM

Whenever doubts, wrong conceptions, or unknowing manifest in our mind, if we can dispel them quickly by gaining a perfect understanding of the actual nature of these objects, this indicates that we have quick wisdom.

PROFOUND WISDOM

If we can perfectly understand all the profound meanings of the scriptures without any difficulty, this indicates that we have profound wisdom.

THE WISDOM OF EXPOUNDING DHARMA

When we are giving Dharma teachings we need a special wisdom that realizes how much the listeners can understand and which subjects are suitable for them. Moreover we need to understand the correct order of the subjects we are going to talk about – what to say first, what to say next, and so on. We need to understand perfectly the meaning of all that we are going to talk about, and we need to understand special methods, such as suitable analogies and conclusive reasons, that will clarify the meaning for others. In addition we must also understand what qualities we need to become a perfect Teacher, and how to teach the Dharma as explained in Lamrim teachings. The wisdom understanding all of this is the wisdom of expounding Dharma.

THE WISDOM OF SPIRITUAL DEBATE

Since there are so many different views in the world, both religious and non-religious, which are contrary to the views that are presented in the Dharma teachings, we need a special wisdom that understands the methods for dispelling such views through skilful spiritual debate or discussion. In this way we can lead many people to correct spiritual paths, just as Dharmakirti was able to lead many people to correct views by engaging in actions such as spiritual debate.

THE WISDOM OF COMPOSING DHARMA BOOKS

Dharma books are the eyes through which sentient beings can see the spiritual paths to liberation and enlightenment, the light by which they can dispel the darkness of ignorance, and the Spiritual Guide from whom they can receive reliable advice. Therefore, composing authentic Dharma books brings immense benefit to many living beings and causes Buddhadharma to remain for a long time in this world. However, to compose authentic Dharma books we need a special wisdom. We need perfect understanding of the subject matter and the confidence to write about it, and we also need the wisdoms arisen from listening, contemplating, and meditating. With these we can develop the special wisdom that has the complete ability to compose Dharma books.

THE ACTUAL PRACTICE

The actual practice of receiving attainments has seven parts: receiving the attainment of great wisdom, and so on.

RECEIVING THE ATTAINMENT OF GREAT WISDOM

First, by reciting the *Migtsema* prayer we make strong requests to the Venerable Father and Sons so that we may be able to attain the realization of great wisdom. We then imagine white rays of light, which are hollow like straws, coming from the hearts of Je Tsongkhapa and his two Sons and merging into one at the point where the tips touch the crown of our head. We imagine that the great wisdom of the Venerable Father and Sons, in the aspect of orange-coloured nectar, flows from their hearts through the rays of light and enters our body through our crown. Our body is completely filled with nectar, all the atoms of which are in the aspect of tiny Manjushris. From all these tiny bodies of Manjushri, which are the commitment beings, infinite rays of light radiate throughout the ten directions and draw back the great wisdom of all the Buddhas in the aspect of Manjushri's Form Body. These wisdom beings dissolve into the tiny commitment beings within our body and become inseparably one with them. All these countless tiny Manjushris then dissolve into our root mind at our heart. Our root mind and the tiny Manjushris mix completely, like water mixing with water, and we strongly imagine that we have received the great wisdom of all the Buddhas. We meditate single-pointedly on this feeling for a while.

RECEIVING THE ATTAINMENT OF CLEAR WISDOM

We begin by requesting the attainment of clear wisdom by reciting the *Migtsema* prayer. The basic visualization is the same as above, except that this time we visualize the clear wisdom of Je Tsongkhapa and his Sons flowing from their hearts in the form of orange-coloured nectar, all the atoms of which are in the aspect of the tiny letters of Manjushri's mantra: AH RA PA TSA NA DHI. The nectar completely fills our body, and all the tiny letters emanate infinite rays of light throughout the ten directions, drawing back the clear wisdom of all the Buddhas in the same aspect. The wisdom beings dissolve into the commitment beings as before, and then all the countless tiny AH RA PA TSA NA DHI letters dissolve into our root mind at our heart and mix inseparably with it. We strongly imagine that we have received the clear wisdom of all the Buddhas, and meditate single-pointedly on this feeling for a while.

RECEIVING THE ATTAINMENT OF QUICK WISDOM

We begin by requesting the attainment of quick wisdom by reciting the *Migtsema* prayer. Then we visualize the quick wisdom of Je Tsongkhapa and his Sons flowing from their hearts in the form of orange-coloured nectar, all the atoms of which are in the aspect of tiny DHI seed-letters. The nectar completely fills our body, and all the tiny DHI letters emanate infinite rays of light throughout the ten directions, drawing back the quick wisdom of all the Buddhas in the same aspect. The wisdom beings dissolve into the commitment beings as before, and then all the countless tiny DHI letters dissolve

Trijang Rinpoche

into our root mind at our heart and mix inseparably with it. We strongly imagine that we have received the quick wisdom of all the Buddhas, and meditate single-pointedly on this feeling for a while.

RECEIVING THE ATTAINMENT OF PROFOUND WISDOM

We begin by requesting the attainment of profound wisdom by reciting the *Migtsema* prayer. Then we visualize the profound wisdom of Je Tsongkhapa and his Sons flowing from their hearts in the form of orange-coloured nectar, all the atoms of which are in the aspect of tiny Dharma scriptures and Manjushri's wisdom sword. The nectar completely fills our body, and all the tiny scriptures and swords emanate infinite rays of light throughout the ten directions, drawing back the profound wisdom of all the Buddhas in the same aspect. The wisdom beings dissolve into the commitment beings as before, and then all the countless tiny scriptures and swords dissolve into our root mind at our heart and mix inseparably with it. We strongly imagine that we have received the profound wisdom of all the Buddhas, and meditate single-pointedly on this feeling for a while.

RECEIVING THE ATTAINMENT OF THE WISDOM OF EXPOUNDING DHARMA

We begin by requesting the attainment of the wisdom of expounding Dharma by reciting the *Migtsema* prayer. Then we visualize the wisdom of expounding Dharma of Je Tsongkhapa and his Sons flowing from their hearts in the form of orange-coloured nectar, all the atoms of which are in the aspect of Dharma books that we are going to explain. The nectar completely fills our body, and all the tiny books emanate infinite rays of light throughout the ten directions, drawing back the wisdom of expounding Dharma of all the Buddhas in the same aspect. The wisdom beings dissolve into the commitment beings as before, and then all the countless tiny books dissolve into our root mind at our heart and mix inseparably with it. We strongly imagine that we have received the wisdom of expounding Dharma of all the Buddhas, and meditate single-pointedly on this feeling for a while.

RECEIVING THE ATTAINMENT OF THE WISDOM OF SPIRITUAL DEBATE

We begin by requesting the attainment of the wisdom of spiritual debate by reciting the *Migtsema* prayer. Then we visualize the wisdom of spiritual debate of Je Tsongkhapa and his Sons flowing from their hearts in the form of orange-coloured nectar, all the atoms of which are in the aspect of tiny wheels of swords. The nectar completely fills our body, and all the tiny wheels of swords emanate infinite rays of light throughout the ten directions, drawing back the wisdom of spiritual debate of all the Buddhas in the same aspect. The wisdom beings dissolve into the commitment beings as before, and then all the countless tiny wheels of swords dissolve into our root mind at our heart and mix inseparably with it. We strongly imagine that we have received the wisdom of spiritual debate of all the Buddhas, and meditate single-pointedly on this feeling for a while.

RECEIVING THE ATTAINMENT OF THE WISDOM OF COMPOSING DHARMA BOOKS

We begin by requesting the attainment of the wisdom of composing Dharma books by reciting the *Migtsema* prayer. Then we visualize the wisdom of composing Dharma books of Je Tsongkhapa and his Sons flowing from their hearts in the form of orange-coloured nectar, all the atoms of which are in the aspect of tiny Dharma books on the subject upon which we are going to write and tiny wheels of swords. The nectar completely fills our body, and all the tiny books and wheels of swords emanate infinite rays of light throughout the ten directions, drawing back the wisdom of composing Dharma books of all the Buddhas in the same aspect. The wisdom beings dissolve into the commitment beings as before, and then all the countless tiny books and wheels of swords dissolve into our root mind at our heart and mix inseparably with it. We strongly imagine that we have received the wisdom of composing Dharma books of all the Buddhas, and meditate single-pointedly on this feeling for a while.

ATTAINING THE REALIZATIONS OF THE STAGES OF THE PATH

Now, by reciting the *Migtsema* prayer, we make strong requests so that we may be able to attain all the realizations of the stages of the path. Then, while concentrating without distraction on the meaning of what we are saying, we recite the *Prayer of the Stages of the Path* composed by Je Tsongkhapa, known in Tibetan as *Yöntän Zhirgyurma*:

The path begins with strong reliance
On my kind Teacher, source of all good;
O Bless me with this understanding
To follow him with great devotion.

This human life with all its freedoms,
Extremely rare, with so much meaning;
O Bless me with this understanding
All day and night to seize its essence.

My body, like a water bubble,
Decays and dies so very quickly;
After death come results of karma,
Just like the shadow of a body.

With this firm knowledge and remembrance
Bless me to be extremely cautious,
Always avoiding harmful actions
And gathering abundant virtue.

Samsara's pleasures are deceptive,
Give no contentment, only torment;
So please bless me to strive sincerely
To gain the bliss of perfect freedom.

O Bless me so that from this pure thought
Come mindfulness and greatest caution,
To keep as my essential practice
The doctrine's root, the Pratimoksha.

Just like myself all my kind mothers
Are drowning in samsara's ocean;
O So that I may soon release them,
Bless me to train in bodhichitta.

But I cannot become a Buddha
By this alone without three ethics;
So bless me with the strength to practise
The Bodhisattva's ordination.

By pacifying my distractions
And analyzing perfect meanings,
Bless me to quickly gain the union
Of special insight and quiescence.

When I become a pure container
Through common paths, bless me to enter
The essence practice of good fortune,
The supreme vehicle, Vajrayana.

The two attainments both depend on
My sacred vows and my commitments;
Bless me to understand this clearly
And keep them at the cost of my life.

By constant practice in four sessions,
The way explained by holy Teachers,
O Bless me to gain both the stages,
Which are the essence of the Tantras.

May those who guide me on the good path,
And my companions all have long lives;
Bless me to pacify completely
All obstacles, outer and inner.

May I always find perfect Teachers,
And take delight in holy Dharma,
Accomplish all grounds and paths swiftly,
And gain the state of Vajradhara.

After this we recite the prayer for receiving blessings and purifying:

From the hearts of all the holy beings, streams of light and nectar flow down, granting blessings and purifying.

If we combine our Lamrim meditations with this practice we shall gradually accomplish all the realizations of the stages of the path.

CONCLUSION

We begin the concluding stages by imagining that our mind is in the aspect of an orange-coloured letter DHI, which is standing on an eight-petalled lotus and moon cushion inside the central channel at the centre of our heart. We then make the following request:

O Glorious and precious root Guru,
Please sit on the lotus and moon seat at my heart.
Please care for me with your great kindness,
And grant me the blessings of your body, speech, and mind.

We imagine that all the other Buddhas and Bodhisattvas dissolve into Gyaltsabje and Khädrubje, and that the two Sons then dissolve into Je Tsongkhapa. With delight Guru Tsongkhapa comes to our crown where he diminishes to the size of a thumb. We then make another request:

O Glorious and precious root Guru,
Please sit on the lotus and moon seat at my heart.
Please care for me with your great kindness,
And bestow the common and supreme attainments.

After making this request we imagine that Guru Tsongkhapa enters our body and, descending through the central channel, reaches the centre of our throat chakra. We then make another request with the following prayer:

O Glorious and precious root Guru,
Please sit on the lotus and moon seat at my heart.
Please care for me with your great kindness,
And remain firm until I attain the essence of enlightenment.

We now imagine that Guru Tsongkhapa descends to the centre of our heart chakra and dissolves into our mind, which is in the aspect of the letter DHI. Throughout this visualization it is important not to forget the thread of clouds that connects Je Tsongkhapa to Buddha Maitreya in Tushita Pure Land. We recognize that Guru Tsongkhapa at our heart is the synthesis of our mind, Je Tsongkhapa, and our root Guru; and we meditate on this recognition for a while. At this point, if we wish, we can meditate on the Mahamudra that is the union of bliss and emptiness, which is the very essence of Vajra-yana practice.

Finally the eight petals of the lotus, which are the nature of light, close to form the shape of a heart, leaving no gaps between the petals. The heart-shaped lotus is then entirely encircled by the letters: OM AH RA PA TSA NA DHI SU MA TI KIR TI SHI RI BHA DRA AH THI TA NA AH THI TI TE KUR BEN TU, which cover it completely without leaving any gaps. We contemplate that the heart-shaped lotus is now inside the protection circle of the mantra and, if we wish, recite the mantra a few times. Then we finish the session by reciting dedication prayers and auspicious prayers.

THE PRACTICE DURING THE MEDITATION BREAK

During the meditation break we should always remain mindful of Guru Tsongkhapa, who is inseparable from our root mind at our heart. Whenever we eat or drink we should imagine that we are making offerings to Guru Tsongkhapa at our heart; if people make offerings, prostrations, or other gestures of respect to us we should immediately offer these mentally to Guru Tsongkhapa at our heart; whenever we practise any kind of healing or blessing action for the benefit of others we should think that the power of this action comes principally from Guru Tsongkhapa at our heart; and whenever we are in danger or frightened we should immediately remember Guru Tsongkhapa at our heart and recall that he is the nature of Vajrapani. In addition we should continually try to improve our faith in Je Tsongkhapa by contemplating his teachings and his many other pre-eminent qualities.

If we wish to be reborn in Tushita Pure Land easily, it is essential always to remember the thread of clouds that directly connects Guru Tsongkhapa at our heart with Buddha Maitreya's heart because this indicates that we have a special connection with Buddha Maitreya. Even if we experience sudden death, providing we remember this thread of clouds we shall definitely be reborn in Tushita Pure Land because our consciousness will follow the pathway of this thread directly to Maitreya's heart. This is an actual transference of consciousness. Thus, if we sincerely practise *Ganden Lhagyäma* and *Migtsema* each day, and remember the thread of clouds at the time of death, we shall definitely be reborn in Tushita Pure Land.

Avalokiteshvara

The Migtsema Prayer

The *Migtsema* prayer is as follows:

> Tsongkhapa, crown ornament of the scholars of the
>   Land of the Snows,
> You are Avalokiteshvara, the treasury of unobservable
>   compassion,
> Manjushri, the supreme stainless wisdom,
> And Vajrapani, the destroyer of the host of maras;
> O Losang Dragpa I request you, please grant your
>   blessings.

As mentioned before, this prayer was composed by Manjushri and revealed in the *Kadam Emanation Scripture*. Je Tsongkhapa extracted it and, changing the first and the fifth lines, offered it as a praise to his Guru, Je Rendapa. Rendapa, however, returned it in its original form to Je Tsongkhapa, saying, 'This is more suitable for you.'

The explanation of the *Migtsema* prayer has two parts:

1 An explanation of the first line
2 An explanation of the remaining four lines

AN EXPLANATION OF THE FIRST LINE

Just as crown ornaments are unequalled among ornaments, so Je Tsongkhapa is unequalled among all Tibetan scholars. There are three ways in which we can understand this:

1 With regard to the pre-eminent qualities of his
   teachings Je Tsongkhapa is unequalled among
   all Tibetan scholars

2 With regard to his practical example Je Tsongkhapa is unequalled among all Tibetan scholars

3 With regard to his Dharma activities Je Tsongkhapa is unequalled among all Tibetan scholars

WITH REGARD TO THE PRE-EMINENT QUALITIES OF HIS TEACHINGS JE TSONGKHAPA IS UNEQUALLED AMONG ALL TIBETAN SCHOLARS

It is only through Je Tsongkhapa's teachings that we can understand the four pre-eminent attributes of the stages of the path: (1) that none of Buddha's teachings are contradictory; (2) that we can take all Buddha's teachings as personal advice and put them into practice; (3) that we can easily realize Buddha's ultimate intention; and (4) that we can naturally become free from the great fault and from all other faults. Although the root text of the stages of the path, Atisha's *Lamp for the Path to Enlightenment* (Tib. *Lam drön*), possesses these four pre-eminent attributes, we cannot discover this simply by reading this text because it is only a few pages long. Thus we need also to study the clear and extensive explanations given in Je Tsongkhapa's Lamrim teachings.

Within Je Tsongkhapa's teachings we find special presentations of how to develop the realization of renunciation, which is the main path to liberation; how to develop bodhichitta, which is the main path to enlightenment; and how to develop the correct view of emptiness, which is the method for eradicating ignorance. These special explanations cannot be found in other teachings.

Without relying upon Je Tsongkhapa's teachings it is difficult during these degenerate times to reach an unmistaken understanding of the precise nature of tranquil abiding (Tib. zhi nä), and actual superior seeing (Tib. lhag tong), or to know how to begin these practices, how to sustain them, and how to complete them. Moreover, without relying upon Je Tsongkhapa's teachings we shall also find it difficult to understand precisely the nature of samsara and actual liberation.

Furthermore, it is only in Je Tsongkhapa's teachings that we find the uncommon, clear, and profound instructions on how the realizations of the four classes of Secret Mantra develop. This is particularly true of the development of the stages of Highest Yoga Tantra: clear light, illusory body, the union that needs learning, and the Union of No More Learning. We can find clear explanations of these profound subjects only in Je Tsongkhapa's teachings.

These pre-eminent qualities of Je Tsongkhapa's teachings are not possessed even by the kings of the Tantras, *Guhyasamaja Tantra* and *Heruka Tantra*, which were composed by Vajradhara, nor by the king of the Sutras, the *Perfection of Wisdom Sutra*.

There are many commentaries to the stages of the path, training the mind, Mahamudra, Tantric practices, and philosophical subjects written by followers of Je Tsongkhapa. These include *Ocean of Nectar*, *Joyful Path of Good Fortune*, *Universal Compassion*, *Clear Light of Bliss*, *Great Treasury of Merit*, and *Guide to Dakini Land*. All of these books are based on Je Tsongkhapa's teachings.

In summary, because Je Tsongkhapa's teachings have no equal in Tibet, Je Tsongkhapa himself is unequalled among all Tibetan scholars. Because a crown ornament is unequalled among ornaments, Manjushri refers to Je Tsongkhapa as the 'crown ornament of the scholars of the Land of the Snows'.

WITH REGARD TO HIS PRACTICAL EXAMPLE JE TSONGKHAPA IS UNEQUALLED AMONG ALL TIBETAN SCHOLARS

There are three different aspects to Je Tsongkhapa's spiritual practice: outer, inner, and secret. With regard to the first, Je Tsongkhapa engaged in all the practices of moral discipline that Buddha taught in the *Vinaya Sutras*, such as the two hundred and fifty-three disciplines of a fully ordained monk. From this point of view he was like a pure Hinayana practitioner who was completely free from the downfalls of the Pratimoksha vows. Because of this, all his bodily actions were immaculately pure and beautiful, and people naturally appreciated him and developed faith in him.

With regard to the second aspect, Je Tsongkhapa engaged in all the practices of moral discipline that Buddha taught in the Mahayana Sutras, and was completely free from the downfalls of the Bodhisattva vows, such as the eighteen root downfalls and forty-six secondary downfalls. All his actions of body, speech, and mind were motivated solely by bodhichitta, and all his daily actions accorded with the Bodhisattva's way of life.

With regard to the third aspect, Je Tsongkhapa engaged in all the practices of moral discipline taught by Buddha in his Vajrayana teachings. As a result of his pure practice of Deity yoga and the yoga of the union of great bliss and emptiness he was completely free from gross and subtle ordinary appearances and conceptions. From Je Tsongkhapa's way of practising the Vajrayana his disciples can clearly understand how to lay the foundation for Vajrayana practice, how to progress in this practice, and how to complete it. They can also realize that the practices of the Hinayana, Mahayana, and Vajrayana taught by Buddha in the scriptures are not contradictory but can all be put into practice by a single practitioner.

In summary, from among all the scholars in Tibet, Je Tsongkhapa showed the best example for practising the Hinayana, Mahayana, and Vajrayana.

WITH REGARD TO HIS DHARMA ACTIVITIES JE TSONGKHAPA IS UNEQUALLED AMONG ALL TIBETAN SCHOLARS

As mentioned above, in *Root Tantra of Manjushri* Buddha predicted that Je Tsongkhapa would perform the deeds of a Buddha. As Buddha predicted, Je Tsongkhapa dedicated all his activities to spreading throughout the world the special Buddhadharma that comes from Manjushri's wisdom. To this end he was tireless in giving teachings on the extensive and profound Dharma, and in writing special Dharma books. So lucid and authentic were his books that even scholars of other traditions praised them. For example, Tagtsang Lotsawa praised Je Tsongkhapa's works as a great treasury of excellent explanation that had never been seen before. Je Tsongkhapa wrote sixteen volumes that clearly reveal the entire Buddhadharma by means of a very special presentation. His writings have exactly the same pre-eminent qualities as his teachings. The main reason why Je Tsongkhapa's books and teachings have such special qualities is that he is a manifestation of the wisdom of all the Buddhas.

To help his special Dharma flourish Je Tsongkhapa established many great monasteries, gathered thousands of disciples who gained advanced realizations, and organized special spiritual programmes in his monasteries. In this way the whole of Tibet was filled with fortunate practitioners who had met Je Tsongkhapa's doctrine.

AN EXPLANATION OF THE REMAINING FOUR LINES

The compassion of all the Buddhas appears in the form of Avalokiteshvara, the wisdom of all the Buddhas appears as Manjushri, and the spiritual power of all the Buddhas appears as Vajrapani. Since Je Tsongkhapa is the synthesis of these three holy beings, if with deep faith we sincerely make requests to him by reciting the *Migtsema* prayer, we shall gain a realization of great compassion like that of Avalokiteshvara, supreme stainless wisdom like that of Manjushri, and great power in destroying obstacles like that of Vajrapani. Gaining these realizations is extremely important for everyone because temporarily they will help us to solve all our daily problems and ultimately they will enable us to attain complete liberation from suffering, and full enlightenment. Realizing this, we should strive tirelessly to make requests to Je Losang Dragpa by reciting the *Migtsema* prayer.

The last four lines can also be understood as follows. The words 'treasury of unobservable compassion' reveal the stages of the vast path, the words 'supreme stainless wisdom' reveal the stages of the profound path, and the words 'destroyer of the host of maras' reveal the stages of the Vajrayana path. With respect to the Buddha families, Avalokiteshvara belongs to the Pāma family, the family of Buddha Amitabha; Manjushri belongs to the Tathagata family, the family of Buddha Vairochana; and Vajrapani belongs to the Vajra family, the family of Buddha Akshobya. From this point of view, therefore, Avalokiteshvara is the vajra speech of the Buddhas, Manjushri is the vajra body of the Buddhas, and Vajrapani is the vajra mind of the Buddhas. Thus, these four lines indicate that if we sincerely make requests with strong faith to Je Losang Dragpa by reciting the *Migtsema* prayer we can easily gain realizations of the stages of the vast path, the profound path, and the Vajrayana path; and through this we can attain the vajra body, speech, and mind of a Buddha. Understanding this, we should strive continuously to practise the *Migtsema* prayer.

We can also apply the explanation of the three ways of making requests mentioned above to these different meanings of the *Migtsema* prayer.

Close Retreat

How to do a close retreat of *Migtsema* has four parts:

1 What is a retreat?
2 The necessary conditions for a close retreat of *Migtsema*
3 The preparations for a close retreat of *Migtsema*
4 The practice of an action close retreat of *Migtsema*

WHAT IS A RETREAT?

On retreat we stop all forms of business and extraneous activities so as to emphasize a particular spiritual practice. There are three kinds of retreat: physical, verbal, and mental. We engage in physical retreat when with a spiritual motivation we isolate ourself from other people, activities, and noise, and disengage from extraneous and meaningless actions; we engage in verbal retreat when with a spiritual motivation we refrain from meaningless talk and periodically keep silence; and we engage in mental retreat by preventing distractions and strong delusions such as attachment, anger, jealousy, and strong self-grasping from arising, and by maintaining mindfulness and conscientiousness.

If we remain in physical and verbal retreat but fail to observe mental retreat, our retreat will have little power. Such a retreat may be relaxing, but if we do not prevent strong delusions from arising, our mind will not be at peace, even on retreat. However, keeping physical and verbal retreat will help us to keep mental retreat, and for this reason Shantideva, in *Guide to the Bodhisattva's Way of Life*, praises the first two kinds of retreat.

A close retreat is a retreat in which we practise special methods that cause us to draw closer to the attainments of a

Manjushri

Tantric Deity. We engage in a close retreat of signs when we remain in retreat until a correct sign of attainment manifests. We engage in a close retreat of time when we do a retreat for a definite period of time, such as six months; or alternatively when we do either a long or short close retreat every year at the same time. There are two kinds of close retreat of numbers: a close retreat of actions and a great close retreat. There are also longer and shorter close retreats of actions. On a long close retreat of actions of *Migtsema* we recite the *Migtsema* prayer four hundred thousand times, and on a short close retreat of actions of *Migtsema* we recite the *Migtsema* prayer one hundred thousand times.

THE NECESSARY CONDITIONS FOR A CLOSE RETREAT OF *MIGTSEMA*

For success in this practice we need to gain at least some experience of the stages of the path so that we have a special motivation of bodhichitta and some understanding of emptiness. We also need strong faith in Je Tsongkhapa and his doctrine, and our daily practice must belong to the pure lineage of Je Tsongkhapa. Upon this basis we need to have received the blessing initiation, or jenang, of Je Tsongkhapa. We also need to understand clearly how to practise this instruction through having listened to or read authentic commentaries.

THE PREPARATIONS FOR A CLOSE RETREAT OF *MIGTSEMA*

We prepare a suitable meditation room, thinking:

> *In each session during this retreat I shall invite Guru Tsongkhapa and all the holy beings to this place; therefore I need to clean my room and prepare special offerings.*

With this motivation we first clean our room and the area around it. In front of statues or pictures of Buddha Shakyamuni, Je Tsongkhapa, and our root Guru, we set out torma offerings and other offerings. We should set up three tormas, for which we can use cakes, honey, biscuits, or chocolates. Since these tormas must remain for the duration of the retreat we should not use substances that perish quickly. In front of the torma offerings we set out two or more rows of offering bowls for the in-front-generated Deities. These should be arranged starting from the right hand of the Deity (our left hand) in the following sequence: nectar for drinking, water for the feet, flowers, incense, light, perfume, and food. Then in front of these we set out another row of offering bowls for ourself, the self-generated Deity, starting from our right hand. Other pure offerings can also be set out anywhere on the shrine.

In front of our meditation cushion on a small table we arrange our vajra, bell, and mala. On the first day of the retreat, before the first actual session, we perform the extensive, the middling, or the condensed Dharma Protector sadhana to prevent obstacles to our retreat. The middling and condensed Dharma Protector sadhanas can be found in Appendix III. Then on the evening of the first day we start the first session of the retreat.

THE PRACTICE OF AN ACTION CLOSE RETREAT OF *MIGTSEMA*

This has two parts:

    1 The practice during the meditation session
    2 The practice during the meditation break

THE PRACTICE DURING THE MEDITATION SESSION

This has three parts:

    1 Preliminary practices
    2 The actual practice
    3 Conclusion

PRELIMINARY PRACTICES

We engage in the practice of *The Hundreds of Deities of the Joyful Land* (*Ganden Lhagyäma*) from going for refuge and generating bodhichitta up to and including dissolving Guru Tsongkhapa into our mind at our heart, by reciting the sadhana *King of the Dharma*, which can be found in Appendix III.

THE ACTUAL PRACTICE

This has six parts:

1 Purifying our body and mind by meditating on emptiness
2 Transforming the basis of imputation for our I by generating ourself as Guru Tsongkhapa
3 Meditating on divine pride
4 Meditating on clear appearance
5 Reciting the mantras
6 The practice of the in-front-generation

PURIFYING OUR BODY AND MIND BY MEDITATING ON EMPTINESS

Having dissolved Guru Tsongkhapa into our mind at our heart, our mind becomes the nature of great bliss. With this feeling of great bliss we imagine that from the heart of Je Tsongkhapa, who is inseparable from our mind, infinite rays of light radiate, pervading all worlds and their inhabitants. These melt into light and dissolve into our body. Our body then melts into light and dissolves into Je Tsongkhapa, who is one nature with our mind. Our mind, Je Tsongkhapa, then becomes smaller and smaller and finally dissolves into emptiness. We perceive nothing but emptiness, and we meditate on this emptiness single-pointedly for as long as possible.

TRANSFORMING THE BASIS OF IMPUTATION FOR OUR I BY GENERATING OURSELF AS GURU TSONGKHAPA

We contemplate as follows:

From this state of emptiness there appears a jewelled throne supported by eight great lions. Upon this, from a letter PAM, there appears an eight-petalled lotus, and upon this, from a letter AH, there appears a moon mandala. In the centre of the moon my mind appears in the aspect of an orange-coloured letter DHI. This then transforms into a sword which is marked by a letter DHI. From this, light rays radiate making offerings to all the Superior beings and fulfilling the welfare of all sentient

Vajrapani

beings. All the rays of light gather back into the sword, which completely transforms and I arise as the great Je Tsongkhapa, the King of the Dharma of the three realms and the essence of all the Conquerors. I have a completely pure body, speech, and mind.

My body, which is made of wisdom-light, is white with a reddish tint. I have one face and two arms, and wear the three saffron-coloured robes of an ordained person and a golden long-eared Pandit's hat. My two hands are at the level of my heart in the gesture of turning the Wheel of Dharma. They hold between the thumbs and forefingers the stems of upala flowers, which blossom at the level of my right and left ears. On the flower to my right is a wisdom-sword, and on the flower to my left is a scripture of the Perfection of Wisdom Sutra in Eight Thousand Lines.

My body is adorned with all the signs and indications of a Buddha, and is clear and translucent, the nature of light. I sit with my legs crossed in the vajra posture in the midst of a mass of brilliant light that radiates from my body.

At the centre of my crown chakra on a lotus and moon cushion is Manjushri, who has an orange-coloured body with one face and two arms; at the centre of my throat chakra on a lotus and moon cushion is Avalokiteshvara, who has a white-coloured body with one face and four arms; and at the centre of my heart chakra on a lotus and sun cushion is Vajrapani, who has a blue-coloured body with one face and two arms. They are complete with all their usual features such as ornaments, clothes, gestures, and implements.

At Manjushri's heart is a white letter OM, at Avalokiteshvara's heart is a red letter AH, and at Vajrapani's heart is a blue letter HUM.

We visualize rays of light radiating from the HUM and inviting Guru Tsongkhapa surrounded by all the Buddhas to come from Tushita Pure Land, and we imagine that they all come to the space in front of us and dissolve into Guru Tsongkhapa. When we say 'DZA' we imagine Guru Tsongkhapa comes to our crown, when we say 'HUM' we imagine that he dissolves into us, when we say 'BAM' we imagine that

Guru Tsongkhapa mixes with us, and when we say 'HO' we imagine that we become inseparably one. Now we strongly believe that our body is the body of the Wisdom Buddha in the aspect of Je Tsongkhapa and that our mind is the mind of the Wisdom Buddha. Focusing on our body and mind, the body and mind of Je Tsongkhapa, we develop divine pride, thinking, 'I am Je Tsongkhapa, the Wisdom Buddha.' At this stage we are no longer using our ordinary body and mind as the basis of imputation for our I, but are using only the body and mind of Je Tsongkhapa. This is the way of transforming the basis of imputation for our I. At this point we need to understand four things:

1 What is the basis of imputation for our I?
2 Why we need to change the basis of imputation for our I
3 How it is possible to change the basis of imputation for our I
4 How to change the basis of imputation for our I

WHAT IS THE BASIS OF IMPUTATION FOR OUR I?

What is a person's I or self? The I cannot be the body and mind because the I is the possessor, and the body and mind are the phenomena that are possessed. For example, when we say 'My body' or 'My mind', this indicates that we regard ourself as the possessor of our body and mind. However, although the I is not the body and mind, when the thought 'I' arises naturally in our mind it does so only on the basis of perceiving our body or our mind. Thus, our body and mind are the basis for imputing our I.

WHY WE NEED TO CHANGE THE BASIS OF IMPUTATION FOR OUR I

When the thought 'I' arises within our mind we automatically develop self-grasping that grasps at the I as existing from its own side. This thought is ignorance. It is the main cause of all the problems we experience and the root of samsara. Because our body and mind, which are the basis of imputation for our I, are contaminated aggregates, whenever we develop the thought 'I' we naturally develop the ignorance of self-grasping at the same time. For as long as we continue to use our present body and mind as the basis for imputing our I we shall never eradicate our ignorance of self-grasping, and so we shall continually have to experience suffering. For this reason we need to change the basis of imputation for our I.

HOW IT IS POSSIBLE TO CHANGE THE BASIS OF IMPUTATION FOR OUR I

In our previous lives we took countless bodies, and each time the basis of imputation for our I changed. When we were born human the basis of imputation for our I was the body and mind of a human, and when we were born as an animal the basis of imputation for our I was the body and mind of an animal. Even within one life the basis of imputation for our I changes many times. For instance, when we were a baby the basis of imputation for our I was a baby's body and mind, when we were a child the basis of imputation for our I was a child's body and mind, and when we grow old the basis of imputation for our I will be the body and mind of an old person.

We may feel that even though we have had all these changes of body there is no problem with regarding them all as our body because they are all of the same continuum; however it is not so easy to understand how another's body, which does not belong to us, can become the basis of imputation for our I. To understand this we can consider the following. When we were conceived in the womb inside the union of our mother's ovum and father's sperm, our body, which at that time was like yoghurt mixed with red liquid, belonged to others. To begin with we had no idea of its being our body, but later, as we became more familiar with its continuum, we came to regard it as our own body and in this way it became the basis of imputation for our I. This clearly indicates that, with familiarity, another's body can become the basis of imputation for our I. In other words, 'my body' and 'other's body' are like 'this mountain' and 'that mountain'; they change depending upon our relative position.

In conclusion, having purified our ordinary body and mind by meditating on emptiness as explained above, we generate ourself as the Wisdom Buddha, Je Tsongkhapa. Then, using Je Tsongkhapa's body generated through our correct imagination as the basis of imputation for our I, we strongly develop divine pride thinking, 'I am Je Tsongkhapa, the Wisdom Buddha.'

HOW TO CHANGE THE BASIS OF IMPUTATION FOR OUR I

We change the basis of imputation for our I by purifying the ordinary appearance of our body and mind through meditating on emptiness and then generating ourself as Je Tsongkhapa as explained above. Then we continually familiarize ourself with the meditations on divine pride and clear appearance. Eventually what was simply imagination becomes an actuality and we experience the pure body and mind of Je Tsongkhapa. This is the special way of changing the basis of imputation for our I through practising the spiritual path. Unlike the normal changes in the basis of imputation for our I which occur from one life to the next due to karma, and which are the very process of samsara, this special method is the means for attaining release from samsara.

MEDITATING ON DIVINE PRIDE

After generating ourself as Je Tsongkhapa in this way, we make offerings and praises to ourself, the self-generated Deity, by reciting from the sadhana. We then engage in meditation on divine pride, contemplating as follows:

Because my ordinary body and mind have been purified I am no longer an ordinary being but Je Tsongkhapa, the Wisdom Buddha. I generated myself as Je Tsongkhapa and invited Je Tsongkhapa to come from Tushita Pure Land to dissolve into me and become inseparably one. Therefore, I am Guru Tsongkhapa, the embodiment of all the Buddhas.

Having strongly generated this special feeling we meditate single-pointedly on it for as long as possible. We need to train in this meditation until we develop strong familiarity with it.

MEDITATING ON CLEAR APPEARANCE

With the divine pride established by the previous meditation we then check precisely our environment and body in order to perceive them clearly in our mind. We try strongly to perceive our environment as Tushita Pure Land, our house as Yiga Chödzin Palace, and our body as Je Tsongkhapa's body, the body of the Wisdom Buddha. We contemplate:

I am sitting on a lotus, moon, and sun cushion on a jewelled throne supported by eight lions. The eight lions are manifestations of my four fearlessnesses in general, and of my four protections that protect sentient beings from the four maras in particular. The lotus symbolizes my complete purity of body, speech, and mind; the moon is a manifestation of my conventional bodhichitta; and the sun is a manifestation of my ultimate bodhichitta. My body is a manifestation of the wisdom of all the Buddhas. My three robes are a manifestation of my realization of the perfection of the three moral disciplines, the long-eared hat is a manifestation of my ultimate view, the two flowers that I hold are manifestations of my realizations of love and compassion, the scripture is a manifestation of my speech, and the sword is a manifestation of my wisdom. My sitting in the full vajra posture symbolizes that I have accomplished the Union of No More Learning.

Through this contemplation we try to perceive a general image of the whole environment, the palace, and the body of ourself, the self-generated Deity, in the aspect of Je Tsongkhapa's body. When we perceive this image we meditate on it single-pointedly.

We train continually in this meditation until we perceive everything, from the environment to ourself as Je Tsongkhapa, clearly in our mind. This is the way to accomplish clear appearance. We can combine this meditation with the practice of

Je Tsongkhapa

training in tranquil abiding, which is explained in *Meaningful to Behold* and *Joyful Path of Good Fortune*.

RECITING THE MANTRAS

Having established divine pride thinking 'I am Guru Tsongkhapa, the essence of all the Buddhas', and the clear appearance of our self-generated body as the Form Body of Guru Tsongkhapa, we then visualize that on a moon cushion at the heart of Manjushri abiding in the centre of our crown chakra there is a letter DHI encircled clockwise by the orange-coloured letters OM AH RA PA TSA NA; on a moon cushion at the heart of Avalokiteshvara abiding in the centre of our throat chakra there is a letter HRIH encircled clockwise by the white-coloured letters OM MANI PÄME HUM; and on a sun cushion at the heart of Vajrapani abiding in the centre of our heart chakra there is a letter HUM encircled clockwise by the blue-coloured letters OM VAJRAPANI HUM PHAT.

We then imagine that infinite rays of light radiate from the letter DHI and mantra at Manjushri's heart and touch the body and mind of all sentient beings. This light purifies the inner darkness of their ignorance, and they attain divine wisdom eyes that can see the reality of ultimate truth and all spiritual paths that lead to liberation. With this visualization we recite OM AH RA PA TSA NA DHI one hundred times. We then imagine that infinite rays of light radiate from the letter HRIH and mantra at Avalokiteshvara's heart and touch the body and mind of all sentient beings of the six realms. The light purifies all their negative karma and causes them to experience uncontaminated happiness. With this visualization we recite OM MANI PÄME HUM one hundred times. Then we imagine that infinite rays of light radiate from the letter HUM and mantra at Vajrapani's heart and touch the body and mind of all sentient beings. The light pacifies all their obstacles to gaining liberation and full enlightenment, and they all conquer the four maras and attain Buddhahood. With this visualization we recite OM VAJRAPANI HUM PHAT one hundred times.

We now imagine that Manjushri dissolves into our body, whereby our body becomes the nature of Manjushri; Avalokiteshvara dissolves into our speech, whereby our speech becomes the nature of Avalokiteshvara; and Vajrapani dissolves into our mind, whereby our mind becomes the nature of Vajrapani.

Then on a moon cushion at our heart we visualize our mind in the aspect of an orange letter DHI encircled clockwise by the *Migtsema* prayer, or mantra. We imagine that infinite rays of light radiate from the letter DHI and *Migtsema* mantra to the ten directions and invite the blessings of the body, speech, and mind of all the Buddhas in the aspect of white, red, and blue rays of light. All these lights dissolve into our mind, the letter DHI at our heart, and we strongly believe that we have received the blessings of the body, speech, and mind of all the Buddhas.

With this visualization we recite the *Migtsema* mantra as many times as we can in each session. For a long action close retreat of *Migtsema* we need to collect at least four hundred thousand *Migtsema* prayers, and for a short action close retreat of *Migtsema* we need to collect at least one hundred thousand *Migtsema* prayers. After reciting these prayers we complete our action close retreat by performing at least seven sessions of the Vajradaka burning offering. In each session we need to collect a hundred Vajradaka mantras together with offerings. This can be done in conjunction with the sadhana in Appendix III.

THE PRACTICE OF THE IN-FRONT-GENERATION

After the mantra recitation in each session we bless the tormas and other offerings and then invite Guru Tsongkhapa together with his retinue to come to the space before us. We strongly believe that Guru Tsongkhapa and all the other Gurus, Yidams, Buddhas, Bodhisattvas, Dakas, Dakinis, and Dharma Protectors are actually present in the space in front; and we offer tormas, other offerings, and praises in accordance with the words of the sadhana.

CONCLUSION

Finally all the other holy beings dissolve into Guru Tsong-khapa, who comes to our crown and diminishes to the size of a thumb. He enters our body, descends to our heart, and dissolves into our mind. We strongly believe that inside the central channel at the centre of our heart chakra, on an eight-petalled lotus and moon cushion, is our mind in the form of Je Tsongkhapa who is inseparable from our root Guru. We concentrate single-pointedly on this appearance for a while. Then we imagine that the eight petals of the lotus close together, forming the shape of a heart without any gaps between the petals. This is completely covered by the letters of the mantra: OM AH RA PA TSA NA DHI SU MA TI KIR TI SHI RI BHA DRA AH THI TA NA AH THI TI TE KUR BEN TU. To conclude the session we recite dedication prayers and auspicious prayers.

In summary, the entire practice, from going for refuge up to the auspicious prayers, can be done in conjunction with the *King of the Dharma* sadhana in Appendix III.

THE PRACTICE DURING THE MEDITATION BREAK

Between meditation sessions we should engage in the practices of the meditation break explained previously. In addition we should maintain three special recognitions: (1) that our environment is Tushita Pure Land; (2) that all its inhabitants and enjoyments are pure; and (3) that we are Je Tsongkhapa, the Wisdom Buddha. If we practise this special way of viewing ourself and others, with a pure motivation, it will prevent us from developing delusions such as anger, attachment, jealousy, and so forth, and it will cause us to be reborn in Tushita Pure Land where we shall meet with Je Tsongkhapa's doctrine and eventually become a Wisdom Buddha.

PART TWO

Relying upon the Dharma Protector

The five lineages of Dorje Shugdän

Introduction to the
Dharma Protector

The practice of relying upon the Dharma Protector is explained in five parts:

1 An introduction to the Dharma Protector Dorje Shugdän
2 The previous incarnations of Dorje Shugdän
3 The nature and function of Dorje Shugdän
4 The benefits of relying upon Dorje Shugdän
5 The way to rely upon Dorje Shugdän

AN INTRODUCTION TO THE DHARMA PROTECTOR
DORJE SHUGDÄN

A Dharma Protector is an emanation of a Buddha or a Bodhisattva whose main functions are to avert the inner and outer obstacles that prevent practitioners from gaining spiritual realizations, and to arrange all the necessary conditions for their practice. In Tibet every monastery had its own Dharma Protector, but the tradition did not begin in Tibet; the Mahayanists of ancient India also relied upon Dharma Protectors to eliminate hindrances and to fulfil their spiritual wishes.

Though there are some worldly deities who are friendly towards Buddhism and who try to help practitioners, they are not real Dharma Protectors. Such worldly deities are able to increase the external wealth of practitioners and help them to succeed in their worldly activities, but they do not have the wisdom or the power to protect the development of Dharma within a practitioner's mind. It is this inner Dharma – the experiences of great compassion, bodhichitta, the wisdom realizing emptiness, and so forth – that is most important and that needs to be protected; outer conditions are of secondary importance.

Although their motivation is good, worldly deities lack wisdom and so sometimes the external help that they give actually interferes with the attainment of authentic Dharma realizations. If they have no Dharma realizations themselves, how can they be Dharma Protectors? It is clear therefore that all actual Dharma Protectors must be emanations of Buddhas or Bodhisattvas. These Protectors have great power to protect Buddhadharma and its practitioners, but the extent to which we receive help from them depends upon our faith and conviction in them. To receive their full protection we must rely upon them with continuous, unwavering devotion.

Buddhas have manifested in the form of various Dharma Protectors, such as Mahakala, Kalarupa, Kalindewi, and Dorje Shugdän. From the time of Je Tsongkhapa until the first Panchen Lama, Losang Chökyi Gyaltsän, the principal Dharma Protector of Je Tsongkhapa's lineage was Kalarupa. Later however it was felt by many high Lamas that Dorje Shugdän had become the principal Dharma Protector of this tradition.

There is no difference in the compassion, wisdom, or power of the various Dharma Protectors, but because of the karma of sentient beings one particular Dharma Protector will have a greater opportunity to help Dharma practitioners at any one particular time. We can understand how this is so by considering the example of Buddha Shakyamuni. Previously the beings of this world had the karma to see Buddha Shakyamuni's Supreme Emanation Body and to receive teachings directly from him. These days however we do not have such karma, and so Buddha appears to us in the form of our Spiritual Guide and helps us by giving teachings and leading us on spiritual paths. Thus, the form that Buddha's help takes varies according to our changing karma, but its essential nature remains the same.

Among all the Dharma Protectors, four-faced Mahakala, Kalarupa, and Dorje Shugdän in particular have the same nature because they are all emanations of Manjushri. However, the beings of this present time have a stronger karmic link with Dorje Shugdän than with the other Dharma Protectors. It was for this reason that Morchen Dorjechang Kunga

Lhundrup, a very highly realized Master of the Sakya tradition, told his disciples, 'Now is the time to rely upon Dorje Shugdän.' He said this on many occasions to encourage his disciples to develop faith in the practice of Dorje Shugdän. We too should heed his advice and take it to heart. He did not say that this is the time to rely upon other Dharma Protectors, but clearly stated that now is the time to rely upon Dorje Shugdän. Many high Lamas of the Sakya tradition and many Sakya monasteries have relied sincerely upon Dorje Shugdän.

In recent years the person most responsible for propagating the practice of Dorje Shugdän was the late Trijang Dorjechang, the root Guru of many Gelugpa practitioners from humble novices to the highest Lamas. He encouraged all his disciples to rely upon Dorje Shugdän and gave Dorje Shugdän empowerments many times. Even in his old age, so as to prevent the practice of Dorje Shugdän from degenerating he wrote an extensive text entitled *Symphony Delighting an Ocean of Conquerors*, which is a commentary to Tagpo Kelsang Khädrub Rinpoche's praise of Dorje Shugdän called *Infinite Aeons*.

The nine Great Mothers

Previous Incarnations of the Dharma Protector

THE PREVIOUS INCARNATIONS OF DORJE SHUGDÄN

The highly realized Master, Tagpo Kelsang Khädrub Rinpoche, composed the following two verses concerning Dorje Shugdän:

> With deep faith I prostrate to you, Vajradhara Dorje
>   Shugdän.
> Although you have already attained the Buddha ground
> And engage in the twenty-seven deeds of a Buddha,
> You appear in various forms to help the
>   Buddhadharma and sentient beings.
>
> You have manifested in different aspects
> As Indian and Tibetan Masters,
> Such as Manjushri, Mahasiddha Biwawa, Sakya
>   Pandita,
> Butön Rinchen Drub, Duldzin Dragpa Gyaltsän,
>   Panchen Sönam Dragpa, and many others.

The meaning of the first verse is quite clear. The twenty-seven deeds of a Buddha are explained in the *Perfection of Wisdom Sutras* and in the eighth chapter of Maitreya's *Ornament for Clear Realization*. These twenty-seven deeds range from showing sentient beings the way to enter the spiritual path to liberation up to guiding them to the final attainment of Buddhahood. Since Dorje Shugdän performs all these twenty-seven deeds it is clear that he is a Buddha.

To guide sentient beings along the spiritual path, Dorje Shugdän manifests many different aspects. Sometimes he appears in a peaceful aspect, sometimes in a wrathful aspect, sometimes as an ordained person, sometimes as a lay person, sometimes as a Bodhisattva, sometimes as a Hinayanist, sometimes as a non-Buddhist, and sometimes even as a non-human.

Since there are so many different emanations of the Buddhas it is difficult to tell who is an emanation and who is not. The only person we can be certain about is ourself; we know whether we are a sentient being or a Buddha, but we do not know about others.

Each Buddha has the ability to manifest as many emanations as there are living beings. This ability is necessary because if Buddhas remained in only one form, without any emanations, they would not be able to help all living beings according to their different needs. Thus, if we refuse to believe that a Buddha can have many different emanations we are indirectly holding the wrong view of denying that Buddhas can help all living beings. In *Meeting of Father and Son Sutra* Buddha Shakyamuni says:

> Buddhas manifest in many different aspects such as Brahma, Indra, and sometimes even as a mara or in the aspect of an evil person – but worldly people do not recognize these emanations.

Buddhas can emanate even as inanimate objects. At one time the great Indian Master, Phadampa Sangye, journeyed to Tibet. When Milarepa heard of this great Yogi's visit he decided to test his realizations. He went to the border and waited for Phadampa Sangye to arrive. When he saw him approaching he transformed himself into a flower to see whether Phadampa Sangye had the clairvoyance to see through his disguise. Phadampa Sangye, however, walked straight past Milarepa, seemingly unaware of his presence. Milarepa thought to himself, 'This so-called Yogi has no clairvoyance', whereupon Phadampa Sangye turned round and kicked the flower. 'Get up Milarepa!' he said, and Milarepa, delighted to discover that Phadampa Sangye was a genuinely realized being, sprang up in his usual form to greet him.

As Tagpo Kelsang Khädrub Rinpoche said, Dorje Shugdän has manifested in many different forms to help living beings. There now follows a brief account of each of the past incarnations of Dorje Shugdän mentioned in the verse quoted above.

MANJUSHRI

At the time of Buddha Shakyamuni, Dorje Shugdän appeared as the Bodhisattva Manjushri, one of Buddha's principal disciples. In reality Manjushri had already attained full enlightenment in a previous age, long before the time of Buddha Shakyamuni. In *Sutra Revealing the Abode of Manjushri* Buddha explains that in the remote past Manjushri had completed the Bodhisattva path and attained enlightenment in his Pure Land as a Buddha called 'Tathagata Lamp of the Nagas'. In the same Sutra Buddha also describes the many different Buddha Lands of Manjushri, and how Manjushri manifests countless emanations to help sentient beings.

Although Manjushri showed the aspect of being a disciple of Buddha, he had great power to help sentient beings. Sometimes people would come to Buddha for help and advice but Buddha would refer them to Manjushri because they had a stronger karmic link with him. Some had such a strong connection with Manjushri that through his blessings and skill they were able to develop very powerful realizations with almost no effort on their part.

One such person was King Ajatashatru, who had committed two particularly negative actions – killing his father and raping a fully ordained nun who was also a Superior being. The consequences of such actions are horrendous. In the *Vinaya Sutras* such actions are called 'actions of immediate retribution' because whoever commits them will definitely take rebirth in a hell realm immediately after his or her death. According to the *Vinaya Sutras* it is impossible to prevent such a rebirth, although it may be possible to shorten its duration. According to the Mahayana Sutras, however, these heavy negative actions can be purified if the correct opponents are applied purely.

 King Ajatashatru developed strong remorse for his negative actions and requested Buddha to give him a special method for purifying them. Buddha taught *Sutra for Eliminating Ajatashatru's Regret* and then suggested that the king seek the help of Bodhisattva Manjushri. Immediately upon hearing this advice Ajatashatru developed strong faith in Manjushri. He invited Manjushri to his house for a banquet, and after the meal he rose to offer Manjushri a very expensive cloak; but just as he was presenting the garment Manjushri disappeared. The king was left wondering, 'Who is Manjushri? Where is Manjushri?' By thinking in this way he realized that he could not find a real, truly existent Manjushri, and he came very close to understanding emptiness. Since Manjushri had disappeared, the king decided to try the cloak on himself; but as he put it round his shoulders he started asking the same questions about himself, 'Who am I? Where am I? Who is the king? Where is the king?' Being completely unable to find a real, truly existent self or truly existent king, he gained an understanding of emptiness. He then entered into meditation and quickly attained a direct realization of emptiness, becoming a Superior being on the path of seeing.

According to the Hinayana teachings, a person who has committed one of the five actions of immediate retribution cannot become a Superior being in that same life, but the Mahayana viewpoint is different. As a result of Manjushri's blessings King Ajatashatru was able to purify his heavy negative karma and attain the path of seeing. Manjushri performed many other special actions such as this.

MAHASIDDHA BIWAWA

Later, to help the Buddhadharma flourish, Manjushri took rebirth as the Mahasiddha Biwawa. Biwawa was born in India, to the east of Bodh Gaya, and joined Nalanda Monastery at a young age. Although he was an emanation of Manjushri and therefore a fully enlightened being, Biwawa studied and practised Buddha's teachings at Nalanda so as to demonstrate a perfect example of how to practise the path to liberation and enlightenment. During the day he studied and meditated on the Sutra teachings, and during the night he practised the yogas of *Heruka Tantra*. As a result of his pure practice he was able to see Vajrayogini and her retinue directly. Whenever he made tsog offerings, Vajrayogini together with fifteen other Dakinis with whom he had a particularly strong karmic connection would come to his room to participate in the feast.

Unfortunately the other monks at Nalanda did not recognize Vajrayogini and the Dakinis but saw them as ordinary women. Believing that he was breaking his ordination vows, they became very critical of him and nicknamed him 'Biwawa', which means 'bad man'. Thinking that Biwawa's behaviour gave the monastery a bad reputation they asked him to leave. Although Biwawa had never broken any of his Vinaya vows he agreed to leave Nalanda, saying, 'Yes, I am a bad man, I will leave.' He handed back his robes, changed into lay clothes, and left the monastery. Then, just like a poor, homeless beggar he began wandering from place to place.

He first went to an area near Varanasi and lived in a cave deep in the forest. The land belonged to a non-Buddhist king who had an intense hatred of Buddhists. One day the king met Biwawa and invited him back to the palace, but when he learnt that Biwawa was a Buddhist he ordered his servants to kill him. The servants first tried drowning Biwawa, but they were unable to pick him up to throw him into the river. They then tried to bury him alive, but he reappeared the next day unharmed. Finally they tried to burn him to death, but again he emerged unharmed. When the king saw that Biwawa was able to protect himself through his miracle powers he developed strong faith in him and in the Buddhadharma, and he and all his subjects became Buddhist practitioners and disciples of Biwawa. This fulfilled a prediction made by an astrologer at the time of Biwawa's birth that Biwawa would become very powerful and, through demonstrating miracle powers, would cause many people to enter the Buddhadharma.

Sometime later Biwawa travelled south to the River Ganges. When he arrived at the river he asked a ferryman to take him across, but the ferryman refused because Biwawa had no money with which to pay him. Biwawa declared, 'Since this river flows continuously, perhaps it is tired and would like a rest' and, causing the waters to part, he walked across to the other side. The ferryman was astounded and asked Biwawa who he was. Biwawa told him a little of his life story, where-upon the ferryman developed great faith and asked to become one of his disciples. Biwawa accepted him as a disciple and gave him many teachings. The ferryman practised diligently and eventually became a highly realized Yogi called Drombi Heruka, one of the eighty-four Mahasiddhas.

Continuing on his travels Biwawa reached a town where he stopped at the local tavern. After he had consumed several drinks the landlady asked him to pay, but Biwawa replied that he had no money. The landlady became angry and threatened him, 'You have until sunset to pay me, otherwise I will call the authorities and have you thrown into jail!' Biwawa promptly used his miracle powers to stop the sun moving and held it motionless for three whole days. The local people were aghast and wondered how such a thing could happen. Finally they asked the king to help them. When the king asked Biwawa what was happening Biwawa replied that he was responsible for the sun not setting. 'If I allow the sun to set,' he explained, 'I shall have to go jail.' The king then reassured Biwawa that if he allowed the sun to set he would not have to pay for his drinks or go to jail. Upon hearing of his reprieve, Biwawa was delighted and immediately allowed the sun to continue its journey across the sky!

As a result of Biwawa's extraordinary deeds many people developed faith in him and in Buddhadharma. In this way he led many people into the spiritual path. When the monks at Nalanda heard of his activities they developed great regret at having expelled him and requested him to return to the monastery, but Biwawa declined their invitation.

SAKYA PANDITA

Biwawa later took rebirth in western Tibet as the great Lama of the Sakya Tradition, Sachen Kunga Gyaltsän, more usually known as Sakya Pandita. Even ordinary beings recognized that he was a very special being. When he was a young child the first language he spoke was not Tibetan but Sanskrit, even though he had never been taught it. He was able to memorize texts even during his dreams. For example, he once dreamt that the great Indian Pandit Vasubandhu was giving him teachings on his text *Treasury of Abhidharma*, and when he awoke he had memorized the entire text, which is almost fifty pages long. Following his Guru, Jetsün Dragpa Gyaltsän, Sakya Pandita studied and practised both Sutra and Tantra and became a great scholar and meditator who was famous for his wisdom and miracle powers.

Sakya Pandita's name spread far and wide, reaching even the Chinese Emperor. The Emperor took a keen interest in Sakya Pandita and invited him to China so that he could meet him in person. He decided to use the visit as an opportunity to check whether or not Sakya Pandita was actually enlightened. He summoned a highly qualified magician and told him to emanate a beautiful palace together with servants, magnificent ornaments, and decorations. Such magicians were very different from those we have nowadays in the West. Through a combination of their concentration, mantra recitation, and special substances they could emanate houses, or even whole cities, for days or months. Unfortunately they did not have the powers to maintain their magical creations indefinitely, and after a while the emanations would disappear. For the duration of their existence however, their emanations seemed to be real, and people would live in them without ever suspecting that they were magically created illusions. The Emperor thought that if Sakya Pandita really was enlightened he would not be fooled by such an emanated palace, but if he was just an ordinary person he would probably think that it was real.

When Sakya Pandita arrived in China the Emperor took him to the emanated palace and asked him what he thought of it, and Sakya Pandita replied that it was very beautiful. 'Do you think this is a real palace?' enquired the Emperor, 'Yes', replied Sakya Pandita, 'Of course it is real.' From this reply the Emperor concluded that Sakya Pandita was not actually a Buddha but just an ordinary being who was deceiving the people of Tibet and China. The Emperor then commanded the magician to re-absorb his emanation, but when he tried to do so he found that he could not. Unbeknown to the Emperor and the magician, Sakya Pandita had used his own miracle powers to transform the emanated palace into a real one! When he discovered this, the Emperor was filled with remorse for having had such negative thoughts about Sakya Pandita. He immediately developed strong faith in him and became one of his disciples. It is said that the palace still exists today as a temple known as 'The Emanation Temple'.

BUTÖN RINCHEN DRUB

Sakya Pandita later took rebirth as Butön Rinchen Drub. He was born in western Tibet near the place where Tashilhunpo Monastery now stands, and was ordained as a monk at an early age. Even while he was a young child his parents realized that he was a very special being. The child would often converse with Manjushri as naturally as he would talk with other people, and it was clear from his speech and his actions that he had already attained great compassion and bodhichitta.

Although Butön did not put much effort into learning Sanskrit he was able to understand it with great ease. He translated Sanskrit texts not previously translated into Tibetan and he corrected many earlier translations. He became a very great and famous Lama, a learned scholar who was wise in both Sutra and Tantra, and he wrote twenty-six volumes of extensive commentaries on subjects from the Kangyur and the Tängyur. Butön's works are so vast that it is difficult for ordinary people to see them as a whole and determine their essential meaning, but they can be clearly understood by following Je Tsongkhapa's elucidations. Butön's works and Je Tsongkhapa's works are very closely related. It is said that if you want to know many different things you should read Butön's books, and if you want to come to definite conclusions you should read the works of Je Tsongkhapa.

Butön mainly emphasized the need to practise Buddhadharma purely. He demonstrated fewer miracle powers than previous incarnations, spending most of his time teaching and writing. At the time of Manjushri and Mahasiddha Biwawa, people generally had more merit and much purer minds, and so displays of miracle powers were often very powerful and effective in causing them to develop faith and other realizations. As times became more degenerate, however, people had less merit and their minds were less pure. For them, displays of miracle powers tended to be counter-productive, giving rise to doubts, scepticism, jealousy, and other negative minds rather than pure minds such as faith. People would even suspect those who displayed miracle powers of using them for selfish or political ends, and those who had dark inner secrets would be fearful of their being exposed. In such situations those who displayed miracle powers would sometimes find themselves in danger of their lives. Moreover there would be a danger that they would attract only disciples who craved miracle powers for themselves. It was for these reasons that Je Tsongkhapa later forbade his disciples to display their miracle powers. The later incarnations of Manjushri, therefore, placed less and less emphasis on miracle powers, choosing instead to help sentient beings by setting a perfect example and giving clear and precise instructions on the path to enlightenment. Thus, realized beings such as Sakya Pandita and Butön Rinchen Drub showed practitioners how to meditate correctly and how to gain experience of the stages of the path, leading them to profound realizations of concentration and wisdom. In this way they tamed the deluded minds of their disciples and led them out of suffering and into pure happiness.

DULDZIN DRAGPA GYALTSÄN

Butön Rinchen Drub was later reborn in central Tibet as Duldzin Dragpa Gyaltsän, who became one of Je Tsongkhapa's principal disciples. Like Je Tsongkhapa he was a very pure practitioner of the Vinaya and so he was called 'Duldzin', which is short for 'dulwa dzinpa', or 'Holder of the Vinaya'.

Although Duldzin showed the aspect of being a disciple of Je Tsongkhapa he was in fact an emanation of Manjushri. Thus, both Teacher and disciple were emanations of Manjushri. From the point of view of ordinary beings this may seem a contradiction but in reality it is not. When he was teaching the Sutras and Tantras Buddha would sometimes manifest as both the Teacher and the principal interlocutors who helped the discourse to evolve. In one of the Tantras Buddha Vajradhara said, 'I am the Teacher and I am the disciple. I am the speaker and I am the listener.' There are Tantras that were requested by Vajrapani, who was an emanation of Vajradhara; and often among the audience there were many other emanations. Since Manjushri is a Buddha he can also manifest countless emanations simultaneously, and so it is not impossible that both Je Tsongkhapa and Duldzin Dragpa Gyaltsän were his emanations.

Duldzin Dragpa Gyaltsän's main activity was to help the teachings of Je Tsongkhapa to flourish. He worked to remove obstacles and to gather favourable conditions for the dissemination of these precious teachings. It was Je Tsongkhapa's wish that the special Dharma derived from Manjushri's wisdom should spread far and wide, and Duldzin, as his devoted disciple, worked tirelessly to fulfil his Guru's wish.

Je Tsongkhapa travelled extensively in response to invitations to give teachings, and also engaged in profound retreats for the purposes of writing and meditating; and while he was away he would leave Duldzin in charge of his affairs. It was Duldzin Dragpa Gyaltsän, for example, who organized the building of Ganden Monastery.

Rather than demonstrating miracle powers Duldzin demonstrated how to practise pure Dharma by relying sincerely upon his Spiritual Guide, maintaining pure moral discipline, and so forth. Like Je Tsongkhapa he showed that there is no contradiction between the external practices of Vinaya, the internal practices of the Bodhisattva path, and the secret practices of the generation and completion stages of Highest Yoga Tantra.

Je Tsongkhapa's disciples believed that Duldzin Dragpa Gyaltsän and Je Tsongkhapa were equal in terms of their realizations, abilities, and wisdom. When Je Tsongkhapa passed away, his throne was offered first to Duldzin, but Duldzin declined the honour and offered it instead to Gyaltsabje, saying, 'You should become the second holder of the Ganden throne. You should teach the Dharma of Je Tsongkhapa and spread it far and wide. I will help your work to be successful by eliminating obstacles and arranging the right conditions.'

PANCHEN SÖNAM DRAGPA

Duldzin Dragpa Gyaltsän was later reborn in central Tibet and became a special Lama known as Panchen Sönam Dragpa. Like Duldzin, he worked to remove obstacles to the flourishing of Je Tsongkhapa's tradition and to gather conducive conditions.

This Lama was unique in that at different times in his life he became the Abbot of Gyutö Tantric College, Ganden Monastery, Drepung Monastery, and Sera Monastery; and while he was Abbot of Ganden Monastery he also became the fifteenth holder of Je Tsongkhapa's throne. In those days the Abbots were elected by the resident monks, and the high esteem in which Panchen Sönam Dragpa was held was demonstrated by his having been appointed Abbot of all four principal monasteries. He is the only person ever to have received this honour.

Panchen Sönam Dragpa wrote many commentaries to both Sutra and Tantra. To this day at Drepung Loseling, the largest Gelugpa monastery, as well as at Ganden Shartse, monks qualify for their Geshe degrees by relying principally upon the works of this great Teacher. He is also highly regarded at other monasteries, such as Sera.

Throughout his life Panchen Sönam Dragpa worked to further Je Tsongkhapa's doctrine. When he became holder of Je Tsongkhapa's throne he composed the following prayer:

So that the tradition of Je Tsongkhapa,
The King of the Dharma, may flourish,
May all obstacles be pacified
And may all favourable conditions abound.

Some time later, when he attended the Mönlam Chenmo, or Great Prayer Festival, founded by Je Tsongkhapa, he composed a special verse of dedication:

Through the two collections of myself and others
Gathered throughout the three times,
May the doctrine of Conqueror Losang Dragpa
Flourish for evermore.

These prayers, which are recited every day after teachings
and pujas at all Gelugpa monasteries and Dharma Centres,
indicate that Panchen Sönam Dragpa's activities were the
same as Dorje Shugdän's – working to cause Je Tsongkhapa's
doctrine to flourish.

Later in life Panchen Sönam Dragpa became the Spiritual
Guide of the reincarnation of the first Dalai Lama, Je Gendundrub, granting him ordination and giving him the name
Sönam Gyatso. It was Sönam Gyatso who visited Mongolia
and so impressed the ruler, Altan Khan, that both he and his
subjects were converted to Buddhism. The Khan gave him
the title 'Dalai Lama', which in Mongolian means 'Ocean
Lama'. Although he was the first to be so called, he became
known as the third Dalai Lama, his two previous incarnations, Je Gendundrub and Je Gendun Gyatso, acquiring
posthumously the titles of first and second Dalai Lama.

When Panchen Sönam Dragpa died he remained in single-
pointed concentration on the clear light of death for fifteen
days. His body then diminished to the size of a forearm and
from this body many statues and relics appeared. From his
manner of dying we can understand clearly that he had
attained the illusory body and was truly an enlightened being.

NGATRUL DRAGPA GYALTSÄN

Ngatrul Dragpa Gyaltsän was the reincarnation of Panchen
Sönam Dragpa. He lived at Drepung Monastery at the same
time as the fifth Dalai Lama, and both these Lamas were
disciples of the first Panchen Lama, Losang Chökyi Gyaltsän.
There is a further connection between these two because
Panchen Sönam Dragpa had been the main Guru of the third
Dalai Lama, and the fifth Dalai Lama was in the same mental
continuum as the third Dalai Lama. Both Ngatrul Dragpa
Gyaltsän and the fifth Dalai Lama were highly respected and
considered to be very pure and precious Teachers.

Ngatrul Dragpa Gyaltsän studied both Sutra and Tantra, mainly under the first Panchen Lama, and became a great scholar and meditator. He went to over a hundred caves to meditate and received many direct visions of Buddhas, Bodhisattvas, and Deities. He made a number of predictions, including one that he would become Dorje Shugdän. Ngatrul Dragpa Gyaltsän died at a relatively young age.

The eight Fully Ordained Monks

The Nature and Function of the Dharma Protector

THE NATURE AND FUNCTION OF DORJE SHUGDÄN

Dorje Shugdän and the Deities of his mandala are the same nature as the Deities of the body mandala of Lama Losang Tubwang Dorjechang, who is in essence Je Tsongkhapa. After Je Tsongkhapa passed away Khädrubje received five visions of him, each time appearing in a different aspect. Later the great Yogi Dharmavajra saw Je Tsongkhapa in the aspect of Lama Losang Tubwang Dorjechang. This name was given to Je Tsongkhapa by Manjushri. It indicates that Je Tsongkhapa is the embodiment of both Conqueror Vajradhara and Buddha Shakyamuni. 'Losang Dragpa' is Je Tsongkhapa's ordained name, 'Tubwang' or 'Powerful Able One' is an epithet of Buddha Shakyamuni, and 'Dorjechang' is Tibetan for Vajradhara. Lama Losang Tubwang Dorjechang is an enlightened being and the principal Field for Accumulating Merit in the Guru yoga of *Offering to the Spiritual Guide*, or *Lama Chöpa*.

In reality the *Lama Chöpa* instruction comes from Manjushri's *Emanation Scripture*, which includes special instructions on Mahamudra. The *Emanation Scripture*, which cannot be read by ordinary beings, was revealed directly to Je Tsongkhapa by Manjushri. It was passed down to successive lineage Gurus, and when it reached the first Panchen Lama, Losang Chökyi Gyaltsän, he extracted the instructions on *Lama Chöpa* and *Root Text of the Mahamudra, the Main Path of the Conquerors* and wrote them down in Tibetan. This was an act of great kindness because it meant that for the first time ordinary beings could read and practise *Lama Chöpa* and the special close lineage of Vajrayana Mahamudra. The Guru yoga of *Lama Chöpa* is one of the most blessed practices within Je Tsongkhapa's tradition, being the essential preliminary practice for

Vajrayana Mahamudra. An extensive commentary to this practice can be found in *Great Treasury of Merit*.

There are thirty-two Deities within the body mandala of Lama Losang Tubwang Dorjechang, and it is these Deities who manifest as the thirty-two Deities of Dorje Shugdän's mandala. This was explained by Je Phabongkhapa, an emanation of Heruka, in his prayer to Dorje Shugdän:

> The aggregates, elements, sources, and limbs of Lama
>   Losang Tubwang Dorjechang
> Appear in the aspect of the five lineages of Dorje
>   Shugdän and their retinues.
> Realizing that in reality I am practising the yoga of
>   the thirty-two Deities of the body mandala,
> I offer this practice to you, O Five lineages of Dorje
>   Shugdän; please accept it with delight.

The way the thirty-two Deities of Dorje Shugdän's mandala relate to the Deities of Lama Losang Tubwang Dorjechang's body mandala is shown in the chart in Appendix II.

Of the Deities of the five lineages of Dorje Shugdän, the principal Deity is Duldzin Dorje Shugdän. He is a manifestation of the aggregate of consciousness of Lama Losang Tubwang Dorjechang. Vairochana Shugdän is a manifestation of the form aggregate of Lama Losang Tubwang Dorjechang, Ratna Shugdän is a manifestation of his aggregate of feeling, Päma Shugdän is a manifestation of his aggregate of discrimination, and Karma Shugdän is a manifestation of his aggregate of compositional factors.

Many sadhanas of Dorje Shugdän state that Dorje Shugdän is the embodiment of the 'Guru, Yidam, and Protector'. Here, 'Guru' refers specifically to Lama Tsongkhapa. Thus, when we practise the sadhana of Dorje Shugdän we are indirectly practising the Guru yoga of Je Tsongkhapa, as well as the practices of Yamantaka and Kalarupa. Atisha used to say, 'Some of you Tibetans have tried to accomplish a hundred Deities but have failed to gain a single attainment, while some Indian Buddhists have gained the attainments of a hundred Deities by accomplishing the practice of just one.' We should bear Atisha's comment in mind and realize that it is much more meaningful to practise one Deity sincerely, regarding that Deity as the synthesis of all Deities, than it is to practise many Deities superficially.

Some people believe that Dorje Shugdän is an emanation of Manjushri who shows the aspect of a worldly being, but this is incorrect. Even Dorje Shugdän's form reveals the complete stages of the path of Sutra and Tantra, and such qualities are not possessed by the forms of worldly beings. Dorje Shugdän appears as a fully ordained monk to show that the practice of pure moral discipline is essential for those who wish to attain enlightenment. In his left hand he holds a heart, which symbolizes great compassion and spontaneous great bliss – the essence of all the stages of the vast path of Sutra and Tantra. His round yellow hat represents the view of Nagarjuna, and the wisdom sword in his right hand teaches us to sever ignorance, the root of samsara, with the sharp blade of Nagarjuna's view. This is the essence of all the stages of the profound path of Sutra and Tantra.

Dorje Shugdän rides a snow lion, the symbol of the four fearlessnesses of a Buddha, and has a jewel-spitting mongoose perched on his left arm, symbolizing his power to bestow wealth on those who put their trust in him. The single eye in the centre of his forehead symbolizes his omniscient wisdom which perceives directly and simultaneously all past, present, and future phenomena. His wrathful expression indicates that he destroys ignorance, the real enemy of all living beings, by blessing them with great wisdom; and also that he destroys the obstacles of pure Dharma practitioners.

Each of the thirty-two Deities of Dorje Shugdän's mandala has a specific function, which are explained in a prayer written by Sachen Kunlo, one of the great Sakya Lamas. In this prayer he explains that the function of Duldzin Dorje Shugdän, the principal Deity of the mandala, is to lead faithful followers to correct spiritual paths by bestowing great wisdom; the function of Vairochana Shugdän is to help us to pacify our negative karma and obstacles; the function of Ratna Shugdän is to help us to increase our good fortune, life span, and virtuous realizations; the function of Päma Shugdän is to help us to control our own mind so that we can help others achieve controlled, calm, and peaceful states of mind; and the function of Karma Shugdän is to overcome the four maras and evil spirits who try to harm faithful disciples. The nine Great Mothers help faithful followers of Dorje Shugdän in their Tantric practices, the eight Fully Ordained Monks help them in their practices of Sutra, and the ten Wrathful Deities aid them in their various daily activities. In these spiritually degenerate times Dharma practitioners experience many obstacles, but if we rely upon Dorje Shugdän with unwavering faith he will care for us just like a father caring for his children.

In general, all Buddhist practitioners need to develop unwavering faith in Buddha Shakyamuni, for without it their Dharma practice will have little power and bring few results; and in particular all Gelugpa practitioners need to develop firm and lasting faith in Je Tsongkhapa, otherwise they will never experience the unique qualities of his doctrine. Faith is the very root of all Dharma experience. Gelugpa practitioners who have a sincere trust in Dorje Shugdän will have no difficulty in generating unshakeable faith in Je Tsongkhapa. Their practice of view, meditation, and action will naturally become pure, and they will easily realize the special uncommon qualities of Je Tsongkhapa's teachings. Thus, they will be able to gain experience of the stages of the path of both Sutra and Tantra without any difficulty.

THE BENEFITS OF RELYING UPON DORJE SHUGDÄN

If we can understand well the nature and functions of Dorje Shugdän we can understand the benefits of relying upon him. Dorje Shugdän always helps, guides, and protects pure and faithful practitioners by granting blessings, increasing their wisdom, fulfilling their wishes, and bestowing success on all their virtuous activities. Dorje Shugdän does not help only Gelugpas; because he is a Buddha he helps all living beings, including non-Buddhists. The sun benefits even those born blind, giving them warmth and ripening the crops that become their food; but should they gain their sight, how much more obvious its benefit would be! In a similar way, although Dorje Shugdän protects even those who do not make an effort to rely upon him, when our eyes of faith in him open and we rely upon him sincerely we shall gradually become more aware of the help we receive from him. If we sincerely wish to experience the benefits of relying upon Dorje Shugdän we must rely upon him constantly over a long period of time, steadily improving our connection with him. In this way we shall begin to notice his beneficial influence in our lives.

We should understand that the principal function of a Dharma Protector is to protect our Dharma practice, not to help our mundane affairs. Bearing this in mind we should not become discouraged if we do not suddenly become very wealthy, for wealth does not necessarily help spiritual practice and can be a great distraction. If we rely sincerely upon Dorje Shugdän he will arrange the conditions that are most conducive for our Dharma practice but these will not necessarily be the ones that we ourself would have chosen! Dorje Shugdän will bless our minds to help us transform difficult situations into the spiritual path, and he will open the wisdom-eyes of his faithful followers, enabling them always to make the right decisions. Although physically they may find themselves alone, inwardly those who put their trust in him will never be apart from a powerful ally and a wise and compassionate guide.

One Lama called Gyara Tulku Rinpoche from Drepung Loseling Monastery wrote a prayer to Dorje Shugdän expressing his gratitude. In this prayer he said:

> First you gave me a highly qualified Spiritual Guide
> Under whom I studied and practised Dharma.
> When through following misleading advice I came
>   close to entering wrong paths,
> You immediately hooked me back into the correct
>   path.

This Lama spent many years in a country where he did not even know the language and where conditions were very difficult. However, he became highly respected and many people sought his wise counsel. He realized that all his spiritual progress, happiness, health, and success came from Dorje Shugdän and not from himself. In the same prayer he wrote:

O Duldzin, King of the Dharma, I thank you for your kindness.
Your body is the synthesis of all Sangha Jewels,
Your speech is the synthesis of all Dharma Jewels,
And your mind is the synthesis of all Buddha Jewels.

The Way to Rely upon the Dharma Protector

The way to rely upon Dorje Shugdän has two parts:

1 The way to rely upon Dorje Shugdän in thought and deed
2 The way to practise the sadhana of Dorje Shugdän

THE WAY TO RELY UPON DORJE SHUGDÄN IN THOUGHT AND DEED

There are two ways to rely upon Dorje Shugdän: in thought and in deed. If we recognize that Dorje Shugdän is the embodiment of the Three Jewels, if we remember his kindness in protecting and preserving the Buddhadharma, if we recall how he eliminates obstacles and gathers the necessary conditions for Dharma practitioners, and if with deep faith we develop respect for him and hold these special feelings continually, we are relying upon Dorje Shugdän in thought.

With deep faith and conviction in Dorje Shugdän we can practise his extensive, middling, or condensed sadhana. After completing a close retreat we can engage in peaceful, increasing, controlling, and wrathful actions and gradually accomplish the supreme attainments. By engaging in these practices we can protect others by helping them to eliminate their obstacles and develop wisdom, to find the right conditions for practising Dharma, to fulfil their wishes, and to meet with success in their daily lives. Whenever we engage in any of these deeds with faith we are relying upon Dorje Shugdän in deed.

There are many commentaries, rituals, and sadhanas in relation to Dorje Shugdän that were composed by high Sakya and Gelugpa Lamas. For beings of this present age the late

The ten Wrathful Deities

Trijang Dorjechang, who was the embodiment of Buddha Shakyamuni, Heruka, Atisha, and Je Tsongkhapa, wrote his great commentary to *Infinite Aeons*, the praise to Dorje Shugdän composed by Tagpo Kelsang Khädrub Rinpoche. He also wrote many special rituals and yogas for gaining different attainments connected with Dorje Shugdän. Through his great kindness and by following his writings, I have had the opportunity to write this short commentary on Dorje Shugdän.

THE WAY TO PRACTISE THE SADHANA OF DORJE SHUGDÄN

There are common sadhanas and special sadhanas of Dorje Shugdän. The common sadhanas, such as the *Heart Jewel* sadhana, can be practised by anyone who has faith, regardless of whether or not they have received a Highest Yoga Tantra empowerment or an initiation of Dorje Shugdän. We begin by practising *The Hundreds of Deities of the Joyful Land*, which is the first part of the *Heart Jewel* sadhana, up to dissolving Guru Tsongkhapa into our heart and reciting the dedication prayers. This practice helps us to make a strong connection with Dorje Shugdän. After this we recite the common sadhana of Dorje Shugdän, with which we make offerings and requests for the elimination of obstacles, and we pray to achieve whatever conditions we need for our practice and for the Buddhadharma to flourish.

If we have received a Highest Yoga Tantra empowerment, we can practise uncommon sadhanas such as the *Wishfulfilling Jewel* sadhana found in Appendix III. Having practised *The Hundreds of Deities of the Joyful Land* and absorbed the Guru into our heart we should generate ourself as our Yidam, invite Dorje Shugdän, and then make offerings and requests according to the words of the sadhana.

In conclusion we need to recognize that all Buddha's wisdom appears in the aspect of Manjushri, that he in turn appears in the aspect of Je Tsongkhapa, and that he in turn appears as Dorje Shugdän. Keeping this recognition in mind we should develop and maintain unchangeable faith in Buddha, Manjushri, Je Tsongkhapa, and Dorje Shugdän.

Dedication

Through my virtues from composing this book with
   pure motivation,
May all living beings throughout all their lives
Never be parted from peaceful and wrathful
   Manjushri,
But always come under their care.

Appendix I
The Condensed Meaning of the Commentary

The Condensed Meaning of the Commentary

The commentary to the sadhana *Heart Jewel*, the essential practices of Kadampa Buddhism, has three parts:

1 The instruction of the Guru yoga of Je Tsongkhapa according to the Segyu lineage
2 Relying upon the Dharma Protector
3 Dedication

The instruction of the Guru yoga of Je Tsongkhapa according to the Segyu lineage has two parts:

1 Introduction
2 The actual practice of the instruction

The introduction has three parts:

1 Je Tsongkhapa
2 The history and lineage of the instruction
3 The benefits of this practice

The actual practice of the instruction has three parts:

1 The actual practice
2 An explanation of the *Migtsema* prayer
3 How to do a close retreat of *Migtsema*

The actual practice has two parts:

1 The practice during the meditation session
2 The practice during the meditation break

The practice during the meditation session has five parts:

1 The preliminary practices of going for refuge and generating bodhichitta
2 Inviting the Field for Accumulating Merit

3 Accumulating merit
4 Receiving attainments by making requests
5 Conclusion

The preliminary practices of going for refuge and generating bodhichitta has four parts:

1 The objects of refuge
2 Generating the causes of going for refuge
3 The prayer of going for refuge
4 Generating bodhichitta

Accumulating merit has eight parts:

1 Requesting the Spiritual Guide to remain for a long time
2 Prostration
3 Offerings
4 Purification
5 Rejoicing
6 Requesting the turning of the Wheel of Dharma
7 Dedication
8 Offering the mandala

Receiving attainments by making requests has two parts:

1 Making requests
2 Receiving attainments

Making requests has three parts:

1 Making requests with regard to Je Tsongkhapa's outer qualities
2 Making requests with regard to Je Tsongkhapa's inner qualities
3 Making requests with regard to Je Tsongkhapa's secret qualities

Receiving attainments has two parts:

1 Purifying impurities
2 Accomplishing wisdom and attaining the realizations of the stages of the path

Accomplishing wisdom and attaining the realizations of the stages of the path has two parts:

1 Accomplishing wisdom
2 Attaining the realizations of the stages of the path

Accomplishing wisdom has two parts:

1 An introduction to the seven types of wisdom
2 The actual practice

An introduction to the seven types of wisdom has seven parts:

1 Great wisdom
2 Clear wisdom
3 Quick wisdom
4 Profound wisdom
5 The wisdom of expounding Dharma
6 The wisdom of spiritual debate
7 The wisdom of composing Dharma books

The actual practice has seven parts:

1 Receiving the attainment of great wisdom
2 Receiving the attainment of clear wisdom
3 Receiving the attainment of quick wisdom
4 Receiving the attainment of profound wisdom
5 Receiving the attainment of the wisdom of expounding Dharma
6 Receiving the attainment of the wisdom of spiritual debate
7 Receiving the attainment of the wisdom of composing Dharma books

An explanation of the *Migtsema* prayer has two parts:

1 An explanation of the first line
2 An explanation of the remaining four lines

An explanation of the first line has three parts:

1 With regard to the pre-eminent qualities of his teachings Je Tsongkhapa is unequalled among all Tibetan scholars

2 With regard to his practical example Je Tsongkhapa is unequalled among all Tibetan scholars
3 With regard to his Dharma activities Je Tsongkhapa is unequalled among all Tibetan scholars

How to do a close retreat of *Migtsema* has four parts:

1 What is a retreat?
2 The necessary conditions for a close retreat of *Migtsema*
3 The preparations for a close retreat of *Migtsema*
4 The practice of an action close retreat of *Migtsema*

The practice of an action close retreat of *Migtsema* has two parts:

1 The practice during the meditation session
2 The practice during the meditation break

The practice during the meditation session has three parts:

1 Preliminary practices
2 The actual practice
3 Conclusion

The actual practice has six parts:

1 Purifying our body and mind by meditating on emptiness
2 Transforming the basis of imputation for our I by generating ourself as Guru Tsongkhapa
3 Meditating on divine pride
4 Meditating on clear appearance
5 Reciting the mantras
6 The practice of the in-front-generation

Transforming the basis of imputation for our I by generating ourself as Guru Tsongkhapa has four parts:

1 What is the basis of imputation for our I?
2 Why we need to change the basis of imputation for our I

3 How it is possible to change the basis of imputation for our I

4 How to change the basis of imputation for our I

Relying upon the Dharma Protector has five parts:

1 An introduction to the Dharma Protector Dorje Shugdän

2 The previous incarnations of Dorje Shugdän

3 The nature and function of Dorje Shugdän

4 The benefits of relying upon Dorje Shugdän

5 The way to rely upon Dorje Shugdän

The previous incarnations of Dorje Shugdän has seven parts:

1 Manjushri

2 Mahasiddha Biwawa

3 Sakya Pandita

4 Butön Rinchen Drub

5 Duldzin Dragpa Gyaltsän

6 Panchen Sönam Dragpa

7 Ngatrul Dragpa Gyaltsän

The way to rely upon Dorje Shugdän has two parts:

1 The way to rely upon Dorje Shugdän in thought and deed

2 The way to practise the sadhana of Dorje Shugdän

Appendix II
The Dharma Protector's Mandala

Appendix II
The Dharma Protector's Mandala

Part of Lama Losang Tubwang Dorjechang's Body	Corresponding Deity of the Body Mandala	Corresponding Deity of Dorje Shugdän's Mandala
The five aggregates	The five Buddha lineages	The five lineages of Dorje Shugdän
form	Vairochana	Vairochana Shugdän
discrimination	Amitabha	Päma Shugdän
consciousness	Akshobya	Dorje Shugdän
feeling	Ratnasambhava	Ratna Shugdän
compositional factors	Amoghasiddhi	Karma Shugdän
The four elements	The four Mothers	The nine Great Mothers
earth	Lochana	Lochana
water	Mamaki	Mamaki
fire	Benzarahi	Benzarahi
wind	Tara	Tara
The five object sources	The five Goddesses	The nine Great Mothers (cont.)
forms	Rupavajra	Rupavajra
sounds	Shaptavajra	Shaptavajra
smells	Gändhavajra	Gändhavajra
tastes	Rasavajra	Rasavajra
tactile objects	Parshavajra	Parshavajra

Part of Lama Losang Tubwang Dorjechang's Body	Corresponding Deity of the Body Mandala	Corresponding Deity of Dorje Shugdän's Mandala
The eight parts of the body	*The eight main Bodhisattvas*	*The eight Fully Ordained Monks*
eye sense power	Ksitigarbha	Ksitigarbha
ear sense power	Vajrapani	Vajrapani
nose sense power	Akashagarbha	Akashagarbha
tongue sense power	Avalokiteshvara	Avalokiteshvara
body sense power	Sarvanivarana-viskambini	Sarvanivarana-viskambini
mental power	Manjushri	Manjushri
veins	Maitreya	Maitreya
joints	Samantabhadra	Samantabhadra
The ten parts of the body	*The ten Wrathful Deities*	*The ten Wrathful Deities*
right hand	Yamantaka	Yamantaka
left hand	Aparajita	Aparajita
mouth	Hayagriva	Hayagriva
right shoulder	Achala	Achala
left shoulder	Takkiraja	Takkiraja
right knee	Niladanda	Niladanda
left knee	Mahabala	Mahabala
crown	Ushnishachakravarti	Ushnishachakravarti
soles of feet	Sumbharaja	Sumbharaja
secret place	Amritakundalini	Amritakundalini

Appendix III
Sadhanas

CONTENTS

Heart Jewel
The Guru yoga of Je Tsongkhapa combined with
the condensed sadhana of his Dharma Protector   111

King of the Dharma
A method for accomplishing self-generation
as Je Tsongkhapa   123

Wishfulfilling Jewel
The Guru yoga of Je Tsongkhapa combined with
the sadhana of his Dharma Protector   137

Vajradaka Burning Offering
A practice for purifying mistakes and
negativities   155

Heart Jewel

THE GURU YOGA OF JE TSONGKHAPA COMBINED
WITH THE CONDENSED SADHANA OF
HIS DHARMA PROTECTOR

Heart Jewel

Going for refuge

I and all sentient beings, until we achieve enlightenment,
Go for refuge to Buddha, Dharma, and Sangha.   (3x)

Generating bodhichitta

Through the virtues I collect by giving and other
    perfections,
May I become a Buddha for the benefit of all.   (3x)

Inviting Je Tsongkhapa

From the heart of the Protector of the hundreds of Deities
    of the Joyful Land,
To the peak of a cloud which is like a cluster of fresh,
    white curd,
All-knowing Losang Dragpa, King of the Dharma,
Please come to this place together with your Sons.

Prayer of seven limbs

In the space before me on a lion throne, lotus, and moon,
The venerable Gurus smile with delight.
O Supreme Field of Merit for my mind of faith,
Please remain for a hundred aeons to spread the doctrine.

Your mind of wisdom realizes the full extent of objects of
    knowledge,
Your eloquent speech is the ear-ornament of the fortunate,
Your beautiful body is ablaze with the glory of renown,
I prostrate to you, whom to see, to hear, and to remember
    is so meaningful.

Pleasing water offerings, various flowers,
Sweet-smelling incense, lights, scented water, and so forth,
A vast cloud of offerings both set out and imagined,
I offer to you, O Supreme Field of Merit.

Whatever non-virtues of body, speech, and mind
I have accumulated since time without beginning,
Especially transgressions of my three vows,
With great remorse I confess each one from the depths of
my heart.

In this degenerate age you strove for much learning and
accomplishment.
Abandoning the eight worldly concerns, you made your
freedom and endowment meaningful.
O Protector, from the very depths of my heart,
I rejoice in the great wave of your deeds.

From the billowing clouds of wisdom and compassion
In the space of your Truth Body, O Venerable and holy
Gurus,
Please send down a rain of vast and profound Dharma
Appropriate to the disciples of this world.

Through the virtues I have accumulated here,
May the doctrine and all living beings receive every
benefit.
Especially may the essence of the doctrine
Of Venerable Losang Dragpa shine forever.

Offering the mandala

The ground sprinkled with perfume and spread with
flowers,
The Great Mountain, four lands, sun and moon,
Seen as a Buddha Land and offered thus,
May all beings enjoy such Pure Lands.

IDAM GURU RATNA MANDALAKAM NIRYATAYAMI

Migtsema prayer

Tsongkhapa, crown ornament of the scholars of the Land
   of the Snows,
You are Avalokiteshvara, the treasury of unobservable
   compassion,
Manjushri, the supreme stainless wisdom,
And Vajrapani, the destroyer of the host of maras;
O Losang Dragpa I request you, please grant your
   blessings.   (7x, 21x, 100x, etc.)

MIG ME TSE WAI TER CHEN CHÄN RÄ ZIG
DRI ME KHYEN PAI WANG PO JAM PÄL YANG
DÜ PUNG MA LÜ JOM DZÄ SANG WAI DAG
GANG CHÄN KHÄ WAI TSUG GYÄN TSONG KHA PA
LO ZANG DRAG PAI ZHAB LA SÖL WA DEB

Prayer of the Stages of the Path

The path begins with strong reliance
On my kind Teacher, source of all good;
O Bless me with this understanding
To follow him with great devotion.

This human life with all its freedoms,
Extremely rare, with so much meaning;
O Bless me with this understanding
All day and night to seize its essence.

My body, like a water bubble,
Decays and dies so very quickly;
After death come results of karma,
Just like the shadow of a body.

With this firm knowledge and remembrance
Bless me to be extremely cautious,
Always avoiding harmful actions
And gathering abundant virtue.

Samsara's pleasures are deceptive,
Give no contentment, only torment;
So please bless me to strive sincerely
To gain the bliss of perfect freedom.

O Bless me so that from this pure thought
Come mindfulness and greatest caution,
To keep as my essential practice
The doctrine's root, the Pratimoksha.

Just like myself all my kind mothers
Are drowning in samsara's ocean;
O So that I may soon release them,
Bless me to train in bodhichitta.

But I cannot become a Buddha
By this alone without three ethics;
So bless me with the strength to practise
The Bodhisattva's ordination.

By pacifying my distractions
And analyzing perfect meanings,
Bless me to quickly gain the union
Of special insight and quiescence.

When I become a pure container
Through common paths, bless me to enter
The essence practice of good fortune,
The supreme vehicle, Vajrayana.

The two attainments both depend on
My sacred vows and my commitments;
Bless me to understand this clearly
And keep them at the cost of my life.

By constant practice in four sessions,
The way explained by holy Teachers,
O Bless me to gain both the stages
Which are the essence of the Tantras.

May those who guide me on the good path
And my companions all have long lives;
Bless me to pacify completely
All obstacles, outer and inner.

May I always find perfect Teachers
And take delight in holy Dharma,
Accomplish all grounds and paths swiftly,
And gain the state of Vajradhara.

Receiving blessings and purifying

From the hearts of all the holy beings, streams of light and
nectar flow down, granting blessings and purifying.

Requests to receive the Guru's blessings

O Glorious and precious root Guru,
Please sit on the lotus and moon seat at my heart.
Please care for me with your great kindness,
And grant me the blessings of your body, speech,
    and mind.

O Glorious and precious root Guru,
Please sit on the lotus and moon seat at my heart.
Please care for me with your great kindness,
And bestow the common and supreme attainments.

O Glorious and precious root Guru,
Please sit on the lotus and moon seat at my heart.
Please care for me with your great kindness,
And remain firm until I attain the essence of
    enlightenment.

Dedication

Through being cared for throughout all my lives
By Conqueror Tsongkhapa as my Mahayana Guru,
May I never turn away, even for an instant,
From this excellent path praised by the Conquerors.

Inviting Dorje Shugdän and his retinue

HUM
I have the clarity of the Yidam.
Before me in the centre of red and black fire and wind,
On a lotus and sun, trampling demons and obstructors,
Is a terrifying lion, which is powerful and alert.
Upon this sits the great king Dorje Shugdän,
The supreme Heart Jewel of Dharma Protectors.
His body is clothed in the garments of a monk,
And on his head he wears a round, yellow hat.
His hands hold a sword and a heart of compassion.
To his followers he shows an expression of delight,
But to subdue demons and obstructors he displays
    a wrathful manner.
He is surrounded by a vast, assembled retinue,
Such as his attendant Khache Marpo and so forth.

Light rays from my heart instantly invite the wisdom
beings from the sphere of nature, and from all the
different palaces where they abide. They become
inseparable from the commitment beings.

Making offerings and requests

HUM
Respectfully I prostrate with body, speech, and mind.
I offer a mass of inner and outer offerings, blissful tormas,
Alcohol, tea, cakes, milk, and curd,
Both actually set out and mentally imagined, filling the
    whole of space.

Commitment, fulfilling, reliance, and appropriate
    substances,
Outer, inner, secret, attractive, and cleansing offerings,
    filling the whole of space,
I offer these to the entire assembly;
May I fulfil the heart commitment and restore my broken
    commitments.

All my harmful thoughts and actions
That have offended your mind, O Great Protector,
I confess from the depths of my heart.
Please purify them swiftly, and care for me with love, like
a mother for her child.

I beseech you from the depths of my heart, O Supreme
Deity,
Please cause the tradition of Je Tsongkhapa to flourish,
Extend the life and activities of the glorious Gurus,
And increase the study and practice of Dharma within the
Dharma communities.

Please be with me always like the shadow of my body,
And grant me your unwavering care and protection.
Destroy all obstacles and adverse conditions,
Bestow favourable conditions, and fulfil all my wishes.

Now is the time to show clearly your versatile strength
Through your four actions, which are swift, incisive, and
unobstructed,
To fulfil quickly my special heartfelt desires
In accordance with my wishes;

Now is the time to distinguish the truth and falsity of
actions and effects;
Now is the time to dispel false accusations against the
innocent;
Now is the time to protect the pitiful and protectorless;
Now is the time to protect Dharma practitioners as your
children.

In short, from now until I attain the essence of
enlightenment,
I shall honour you as the embodiment of my Guru, Deity,
and Protector.
Therefore please watch over me during the three periods
of the day and the night
And never waver in your actions as my Protector.

Requesting the fulfilment of wishes

HUM
Whenever your followers with commitments
Request any of the four actions,
Swiftly, incisively, and without delay, you show signs for
all to see;
So please accomplish the actions that I now request of you.

The stainless sun of Je Tsongkhapa's tradition
Shines throughout the sky of samsara and nirvana,
Eliminating the darkness of inferior and wrong paths;
Please cause its light to spread and bring good fortune to
all living beings.

May the glorious Gurus who uphold this tradition
Have indestructible lives, as stable as the supreme victory
banner;
May they send down a rain of deeds fulfilling the wishes
of disciples,
So that Je Tsongkhapa's doctrine will flourish.

Through increasing the study, practice, pure discipline,
and harmony
Of the communities who uphold the stainless doctrine of
Buddha,
And who keep moral discipline with pure minds,
Please cause the Gedän tradition to increase like a waxing
moon.

Through your actions please fulfil the essential wishes
Of all practitioners who uphold the victory banner
Of practising single-pointedly the stages of the paths of
Sutra and Tantra,
The essence of all the teachings they have heard.

Beings throughout this great earth are engaged in
different actions
Of Dharma, non-Dharma, happiness, suffering, cause and
effect;

Through your skilful deeds of preventing and nurturing,
Please lead all beings into the good path to ultimate
  happiness.

In particular, please destroy the obstacles and unfavourable
  conditions
Of myself and other practitioners.
Increase our lives, our merit, and our resources,
And gather all things animate and inanimate to be freely
  enjoyed.

Please be with me always like the shadow of my body,
And care for me always like a friend,
By accomplishing swiftly whatever I wish for,
And whatever I ask of you.

Please perform immediately, without delaying for a year,
  or even for a month,
Appropriate actions to eliminate all obstacles
Caused by misguided beings with harmful minds who try
  to destroy Je Tsongkhapa's doctrine,
And especially by those who try to harm practitioners.

Please remain in this place always, surrounded by most
  excellent enjoyments.
As my guest, partake continuously of tormas and offerings;
And since you are entrusted with the protection of human
  wealth and enjoyments,
Never waver as my guardian throughout the day and the
  night.

All the attainments I desire
Arise from merely remembering you.
O Wishfulfilling Jewel, Protector of the Dharma,
Please accomplish all my wishes.   (3x)

Dedication

By this virtue may I quickly
Attain the enlightened state of the Guru,
And then lead every living being
Without exception to that ground.

Through my virtues from practising with pure motivation,
May all living beings throughout all their lives
Never be parted from peaceful and wrathful Manjushri,
But always come under their care.

Prayers for the Virtuous Tradition

So that the tradition of Je Tsongkhapa,
The King of the Dharma, may flourish,
May all obstacles be pacified
And may all favourable conditions abound.

Through the two collections of myself and others
Gathered throughout the three times,
May the doctrine of Conqueror Losang Dragpa
Flourish for evermore.

Migtsema prayer

MIG ME TSE WAI TER CHEN CHÄN RÄ ZIG
DRI ME KHYEN PAI WANG PO JAM PÄL YANG
GANG CHÄN KHÄ WAI TSUG GYÄN TSONG KHA PA
LO ZANG DRAG PAI ZHAB LA SÖL WA DEB   (3x)

Colophon: This practice was compiled from traditional sources
by Venerable Geshe Kelsang Gyatso Rinpoche.

King of the Dharma

A METHOD FOR ACCOMPLISHING
SELF-GENERATION AS JE TSONGKHAPA

King of the Dharma

Going for refuge

I and all sentient beings, until we achieve enlightenment,
Go for refuge to Buddha, Dharma, and Sangha.   (3x)

Generating bodhichitta

Through the virtues I collect by giving and other
    perfections,
May I become a Buddha for the benefit of all.   (3x)

Inviting Je Tsongkhapa

From the heart of the Protector of the hundreds of Deities
    of the Joyful Land,
To the peak of a cloud which is like a cluster of fresh,
    white curd,
All-knowing Losang Dragpa, King of the Dharma,
Please come to this place together with your Sons.

Prayer of seven limbs

In the space before me on a lion throne, lotus, and moon,
The venerable Gurus smile with delight.
O Supreme Field of Merit for my mind of faith,
Please remain for a hundred aeons to spread the doctrine.

Your mind of wisdom realizes the full extent of objects of
    knowledge,
Your eloquent speech is the ear-ornament of the fortunate,
Your beautiful body is ablaze with the glory of renown,
I prostrate to you, whom to see, to hear, and to remember
    is so meaningful.

Pleasing water offerings, various flowers,
Sweet-smelling incense, lights, scented water, and so forth,
A vast cloud of offerings both set out and imagined,
I offer to you, O Supreme Field of Merit.

Whatever non-virtues of body, speech, and mind
I have accumulated since time without beginning,
Especially transgressions of my three vows,
With great remorse I confess each one from the depths of
my heart.

In this degenerate age you strove for much learning and
accomplishment.
Abandoning the eight worldly concerns, you made your
freedom and endowment meaningful.
O Protector, from the very depths of my heart,
I rejoice in the great wave of your deeds.

From the billowing clouds of wisdom and compassion
In the space of your Truth Body, O Venerable and holy
Gurus,
Please send down a rain of vast and profound Dharma
Appropriate to the disciples of this world.

Through the virtues I have accumulated here,
May the doctrine and all living beings receive every
benefit.
Especially may the essence of the doctrine
Of Venerable Losang Dragpa shine forever.

Offering the mandala

The ground sprinkled with perfume and spread with
flowers,
The Great Mountain, four lands, sun and moon,
Seen as a Buddha Land and offered thus,
May all beings enjoy such Pure Lands.

IDAM GURU RATNA MANDALAKAM NIRYATAYAMI

Migtsema prayer

Tsongkhapa, crown ornament of the scholars of the Land
of the Snows,
You are Avalokiteshvara, the treasury of unobservable
compassion,
Manjushri, the supreme stainless wisdom,
And Vajrapani, the destroyer of the host of maras;
O Losang Dragpa I request you, please grant your
blessings.   (7x, 21x, 100x, etc.)

MIG ME TSE WAI TER CHEN CHÄN RÄ ZIG
DRI ME KHYEN PAI WANG PO JAM PÄL YANG
DÜ PUNG MA LÜ JOM DZÄ SANG WAI DAG
GANG CHÄN KHÄ WAI TSUG GYÄN TSONG KHA PA
LO ZANG DRAG PAI ZHAB LA SÖL WA DEB

Requests to receive the Guru's blessings

O Glorious and precious root Guru,
Please sit on the lotus and moon seat at my heart.
Please care for me with your great kindness,
And grant me the blessings of your body, speech,
and mind.

O Glorious and precious root Guru,
Please sit on the lotus and moon seat at my heart.
Please care for me with your great kindness,
And bestow the common and supreme attainments.

O Glorious and precious root Guru,
Please sit on the lotus and moon seat at my heart.
Please care for me with your great kindness,
And remain firm until I attain the essence of
enlightenment.

Self-generation as Je Tsongkhapa

OM SÖBHAWA SHUDDHA SARWA DHARMA SÖBHAWA
SHUDDHO HAM
OM SHUNYATA GYANA VAJRA SÖBHAWA ÄMAKO HAM
Everything becomes emptiness.

The letter DHI

From the state of emptiness, in my place, there appears
a jewelled throne supported by eight great lions. Upon
this from PAM comes a lotus and from AH comes a moon.
Upon this my mind appears as an orange letter DHI,
which transforms into a sword marked by a letter DHI.

From this light rays radiate making offerings to the
Superior beings and fulfilling the welfare of sentient
beings. Gathering back they completely transform and
I arise as the great Tsongkhapa, the King of the Dharma
of the three realms and the essence of all the Conquerors.
I have a completely pure body, speech, and mind.

I have a white-coloured body, one face, and two hands.
My body is clothed in the three saffron robes of an
ordained person, and on my head I wear a golden
long-eared Pandit's hat. My hands, at the level of my
heart in the gesture of turning the Wheel of Dharma,
hold between the thumbs and forefingers the stems of
upala flowers, which blossom at the level of my right and
left ears. On the right flower is a wisdom-sword and on
the left is a scripture of the *Perfection of Wisdom Sutra in
Eight Thousand Lines*.

My body is adorned with the signs and indications of a
Buddha, and is clear and translucent, the nature of light.
I sit with my legs crossed in the vajra posture in the centre
of a mass of light that radiates from my body.

At the centre of my crown chakra on a lotus and moon
cushion is Manjushri, who is orange in colour with one
face and two arms. At the centre of my throat chakra on a
lotus and moon cushion is Avalokiteshvara, who is white
in colour with one face and four arms. At the centre of my
heart chakra on a lotus and sun cushion is Vajrapani, who
is blue in colour with one face and two arms. They are
complete with their usual features such as ornaments,
clothes, gestures, and implements.

At the heart of Manjushri is a white letter OM, at the heart of Avalokiteshvara is a red letter AH, and at the heart of Vajrapani is a blue letter HUM.

From the HUM at my heart light rays radiate inviting the great Tsongkhapa, the King of the Dharma, to come from Tushita Pure Land.

DZA HUM BAM HO
We become non-dual.

Blessing the offerings to the self-generated Deity

OM VAJRA AMRITA KUNDALI HANA HANA HUM PHAT
OM SÖBHAWA SHUDDHA SARWA DHARMA SÖBHAWA
   SHUDDHO HAM
Everything becomes emptiness.

From the state of emptiness, from DHRUM letters come broad and expansive jewelled vessels. Inside each of these there is a letter OM, which melts into light and there arise heavenly offering substances.

OM AHRGHAM AH HUM
OM PADÄM AH HUM
OM PUPE AH HUM
OM DHUPE AH HUM
OM ALOKE AH HUM
OM GÄNDHE AH HUM
OM NEWIDE AH HUM
OM SHAPTA AH HUM

Making offerings to the self-generated Deity

OM GURU SUMATI KIRTI AHRGHAM PARTITZA HUM SÖHA
OM GURU SUMATI KIRTI PADÄM PARTITZA HUM SÖHA
OM GURU SUMATI KIRTI PUPE PARTITZA HUM SÖHA
OM GURU SUMATI KIRTI DHUPE PARTITZA HUM SÖHA
OM GURU SUMATI KIRTI ALOKE PARTITZA HUM SÖHA
OM GURU SUMATI KIRTI GÄNDHE PARTITZA HUM SÖHA
OM GURU SUMATI KIRTI NEWIDE PARTITZA HUM SÖHA
OM GURU SUMATI KIRTI SHAPTA PARTITZA HUM SÖHA

Praise to the self-generated Deity

I prostrate to you, O Glorious and venerable precious Guru,
Who are kinder than all the Buddhas,
The sole eyes of migrating beings of the three realms,
And the Protector of all those who seek liberation.

Meditating on divine pride and clear appearance

At this point we meditate on divine pride and clear appearance according to the commentary.

Reciting the mantras

On a moon cushion at the heart of Manjushri abiding at the centre of my crown chakra is a letter DHI encircled clockwise by the orange letters OM AH RA PA TSA NA. On a moon cushion at the heart of Avalokiteshvara abiding at the centre of my throat chakra is a letter HRIH encircled clockwise by the white letters OM MANI PÄME HUM. On a sun cushion at the heart of Vajrapani abiding at the centre of my heart chakra is a letter HUM encircled clockwise by the blue letters OM VAJRAPANI HUM PHAT.

From the letter DHI and the mantra at Manjushri's heart infinite rays of light radiate and touch the body and mind of all sentient beings. The light purifies the inner darkness of their ignorance and they attain divine wisdom eyes.

OM AH RA PA TSA NA DHI   (100x)

From the letter HRIH and the mantra at Avalokiteshvara's heart infinite rays of light radiate and touch the body and mind of all sentient beings of the six realms. The light purifies all their negative karma and they experience uncontaminated happiness.

OM MANI PÄME HUM   (100x)

From the letter HUM and the mantra at Vajrapani's heart infinite rays of light radiate and touch the body and mind of all sentient beings. The light pacifies all their obstacles to gaining liberation and full enlightenment, and they all conquer the four maras and attain Buddhahood.

OM VAJRAPANI HUM PHAT   (100x)

Manjushri dissolves into my body whereby my body becomes the nature of Manjushri; Avalokiteshvara dissolves into my speech whereby my speech becomes the nature of Avalokiteshvara; and Vajrapani dissolves into my mind whereby my mind becomes the nature of Vajrapani.

Actual recitation of the *Migtsema* mantra

On a moon cushion at my heart, my mind appears in the aspect of an orange letter DHI encircled clockwise by the *Migtsema* mantra. From the mantra and letter DHI infinite rays of light radiate to the ten directions, drawing back the blessings of the body, speech, and mind of all the Buddhas in the aspect of white, red, and blue rays of light. These dissolve into my mind, the letter DHI at my heart, and I receive the blessings of the body, speech, and mind of all the Buddhas.

Tsongkhapa, crown ornament of the scholars of the Land
  of the Snows,
You are Avalokiteshvara, the treasury of unobservable
  compassion,
Manjushri, the supreme stainless wisdom,
And Vajrapani, the destroyer of the host of maras;
O Losang Dragpa I request you, please grant your
  blessings.

MIG ME TSE WAI TER CHEN CHÄN RÄ ZIG
DRI ME KHYEN PAI WANG PO JAM PÄL YANG
DÜ PUNG MA LÜ JOM DZÄ SANG WAI DAG
GANG CHÄN KHÄ WAI TSUG GYÄN TSONG KHA PA
LO ZANG DRAG PAI ZHAB LA SÖL WA DEB

Recite as many times as you wish.

Blessing the offerings to the in-front-generation

OM VAJRA AMRITA KUNDALI HANA HANA HUM PHAT
OM SÖBHAWA SHUDDHA SARWA DHARMA SÖBHAWA
SHUDDHO HAM
Everything becomes emptiness.

From the state of emptiness, from DHRUM letters come
broad and expansive jewelled vessels. Inside each of these
there is a letter OM which melts into light and there arise
heavenly offering substances.

OM AHRGHAM AH HUM
OM PADÄM AH HUM
OM PUPE AH HUM
OM DHUPE AH HUM
OM ALOKE AH HUM
OM GÄNDHE AH HUM
OM NEWIDE AH HUM
OM SHAPTA AH HUM

Blessing the torma

OM VAJRA AMRITA KUNDALI HANA HANA HUM PHAT
OM SÖBHAWA SHUDDHA SARWA DHARMA SÖBHAWA
SHUDDHO HAM
Everything becomes emptiness.

From the state of emptiness, from a DHRUM before me
comes a broad and expansive jewelled vessel. Inside from
a letter OM comes a torma, a vast ocean of uncontaminated
nectar of exalted wisdom, which is brilliant and pervasive.
OM AH HUM   (3x)

Inviting the guests of the torma offering

From the letter DHI at my heart light rays radiate and
invite the King of the Dharma, the great Tsongkhapa,
surrounded by the assembly of Buddhas and Bodhisattvas,
to come to the space before me. They partake of the
essence of the torma by drawing it through their tongues,
which are straws of vajra light.

Actual torma offering

OM GURU SUMATI KIRTI SAPARIWARA IDAM BALINGTA
  KHA KHA KHAHI KHAHI   (3x)

Making offerings

OM GURU SUMATI KIRTI AHRGHAM PARTITZA HUM SÖHA
OM GURU SUMATI KIRTI PADÄM PARTITZA HUM SÖHA
OM GURU SUMATI KIRTI PUPE PARTITZA HUM SÖHA
OM GURU SUMATI KIRTI DHUPE PARTITZA HUM SÖHA
OM GURU SUMATI KIRTI ALOKE PARTITZA HUM SÖHA
OM GURU SUMATI KIRTI GÄNDHE PARTITZA HUM SÖHA
OM GURU SUMATI KIRTI NEWIDE PARTITZA HUM SÖHA
OM GURU SUMATI KIRTI SHAPTA PARTITZA HUM SÖHA

Praise

I prostrate to you, O Glorious and venerable precious
  Guru,
Who are kinder than all the Buddhas,
The sole eyes of migrating beings of the three realms,
And the Protector of all those who seek liberation.

Requesting forbearance

OM VAJRA SATTÖ AH   (3x)

Whatever mistakes I have made
Through not finding, not understanding,
Or not having the ability,
Please, O Protector, be patient with all of these.

Dissolving Guru Tsongkhapa into our heart

The holy beings, guests of the torma offering, dissolve into
Guru Tsongkhapa, and he dissolves into my mind, which
is in the aspect of Je Tsongkhapa at my heart.

Dedication

Thus, through my virtues from making offerings and
   requests
To the Venerable Guru, the source of all attainments,
May I always come under the special care
Of Guru Manjushri throughout all my lives.

Through meditating on Buddha Maitreya
And the precious Tushita Pure Land,
May I accomplish that Pure Land and take rebirth there
Immediately after this life.

Through inviting the Venerable Guru and his two Sons
From Maitreya's heart to the peak of a cloud,
And accumulating merit through the seven limbs,
May I easily ripen all my virtuous seeds.

Through my practice of the *Migtsema* prayer
With the strong recognition of Guru Tsongkhapa
As the embodiment of the three holy beings,
May all living beings attain the holy state of a Buddha.

Auspicious prayer

When I meet the holy Dharma of Je Tsongkhapa
And practise sincerely by means of the ten Dharma actions,
May all the powerful Dharma Protectors assist me,
And may a great ocean of auspiciousness pervade all
   directions.

Prayers for the Virtuous Tradition

So that the tradition of Je Tsongkhapa,
The King of the Dharma, may flourish,
May all obstacles be pacified
And may all favourable conditions abound.

Through the two collections of myself and others
Gathered throughout the three times,
May the doctrine of Conqueror Losang Dragpa
Flourish for evermore.

Migtsema prayer

MIG ME TSE WAI TER CHEN CHÄN RÄ ZIG
DRI ME KHYEN PAI WANG PO JAM PÄL YANG
GANG CHÄN KHÄ WAI TSUG GYÄN TSONG KHA PA
LO ZANG DRAG PAI ZHAB LA SÖL WA DEB   (3x)

Colophon: This sadhana was composed by Venerable
Geshe Kelsang Gyatso Rinpoche.

Wishfulfilling Jewel

THE GURU YOGA OF JE TSONGKHAPA
COMBINED WITH THE SADHANA OF
HIS DHARMA PROTECTOR

Wishfulfilling Jewel

Going for refuge

I and all sentient beings, until we achieve enlightenment,
Go for refuge to Buddha, Dharma, and Sangha.   (3x)

Generating bodhichitta

Through the virtues I collect by giving and other
  perfections,
May I become a Buddha for the benefit of all.   (3x)

Inviting Je Tsongkhapa

From the heart of the Protector of the hundreds of Deities
  of the Joyful Land,
To the peak of a cloud which is like a cluster of fresh,
  white curd,
All-knowing Losang Dragpa, King of the Dharma,
Please come to this place together with your Sons.

Prayer of seven limbs

In the space before me on a lion throne, lotus, and moon,
The venerable Gurus smile with delight.
O Supreme Field of Merit for my mind of faith,
Please remain for a hundred aeons to spread the doctrine.

Your mind of wisdom realizes the full extent of objects of
  knowledge,
Your eloquent speech is the ear-ornament of the fortunate,
Your beautiful body is ablaze with the glory of renown,
I prostrate to you, whom to see, to hear, and to remember
  is so meaningful.

Pleasing water offerings, various flowers,
Sweet-smelling incense, lights, scented water, and so forth,
A vast cloud of offerings both set out and imagined,
I offer to you, O Supreme Field of Merit.

Whatever non-virtues of body, speech, and mind
I have accumulated since time without beginning,
Especially transgressions of my three vows,
With great remorse I confess each one from the depths of
  my heart.

In this degenerate age you strove for much learning and
  accomplishment.
Abandoning the eight worldly concerns, you made your
  freedom and endowment meaningful.
O Protector, from the very depths of my heart,
I rejoice in the great wave of your deeds.

From the billowing clouds of wisdom and compassion
In the space of your Truth Body, O Venerable and holy
  Gurus,
Please send down a rain of vast and profound Dharma
Appropriate to the disciples of this world.

Through the virtues I have accumulated here,
May the doctrine and all living beings receive every
  benefit.
Especially may the essence of the doctrine
Of Venerable Losang Dragpa shine forever.

Offering the mandala

The ground sprinkled with perfume and spread with
  flowers,
The Great Mountain, four lands, sun and moon,
Seen as a Buddha Land and offered thus,
May all beings enjoy such Pure Lands.

IDAM GURU RATNA MANDALAKAM NIRYATAYAMI

Migtsema prayer

Tsongkhapa, crown ornament of the scholars of the Land
  of the Snows,
You are Avalokiteshvara, the treasury of unobservable
  compassion,
Manjushri, the supreme stainless wisdom,
And Vajrapani, the destroyer of the host of maras;
O Losang Dragpa I request you, please grant your
  blessings.   (7x, 21x, 100x, etc.)

MIG ME TSE WAI TER CHEN CHÄN RÄ ZIG
DRI ME KHYEN PAI WANG PO JAM PÄL YANG
DÜ PUNG MA LÜ JOM DZÄ SANG WAI DAG
GANG CHÄN KHÄ WAI TSUG GYÄN TSONG KHA PA
LO ZANG DRAG PAI ZHAB LA SÖL WA DEB

Prayer of the Stages of the Path

The path begins with strong reliance
On my kind Teacher, source of all good;
O Bless me with this understanding
To follow him with great devotion.

This human life with all its freedoms,
Extremely rare, with so much meaning;
O Bless me with this understanding
All day and night to seize its essence.

My body, like a water bubble,
Decays and dies so very quickly;
After death come results of karma,
Just like the shadow of a body.

With this firm knowledge and remembrance
Bless me to be extremely cautious,
Always avoiding harmful actions
And gathering abundant virtue.

Samsara's pleasures are deceptive,
Give no contentment, only torment;
So please bless me to strive sincerely
To gain the bliss of perfect freedom.

O Bless me so that from this pure thought
Come mindfulness and greatest caution,
To keep as my essential practice
The doctrine's root, the Pratimoksha.

Just like myself all my kind mothers
Are drowning in samsara's ocean;
O So that I may soon release them,
Bless me to train in bodhichitta.

But I cannot become a Buddha
By this alone without three ethics;
So bless me with the strength to practise
The Bodhisattva's ordination.

By pacifying my distractions
And analyzing perfect meanings,
Bless me to quickly gain the union
Of special insight and quiescence.

When I become a pure container
Through common paths, bless me to enter
The essence practice of good fortune,
The supreme vehicle, Vajrayana.

The two attainments both depend on
My sacred vows and my commitments;
Bless me to understand this clearly
And keep them at the cost of my life.

By constant practice in four sessions,
The way explained by holy Teachers,
O Bless me to gain both the stages
Which are the essence of the Tantras.

May those who guide me on the good path
And my companions all have long lives;
Bless me to pacify completely
All obstacles, outer and inner.

May I always find perfect Teachers
And take delight in holy Dharma,
Accomplish all grounds and paths swiftly,
And gain the state of Vajradhara.

Receiving blessings and purifying

From the hearts of all the holy beings, streams of light and nectar flow down, granting blessings and purifying.

Requests to receive the Guru's blessings

O Glorious and precious root Guru,
Please sit on the lotus and moon seat at my heart.
Please care for me with your great kindness,
And grant me the blessings of your body, speech,
   and mind.

O Glorious and precious root Guru,
Please sit on the lotus and moon seat at my heart.
Please care for me with your great kindness,
And bestow the common and supreme attainments.

O Glorious and precious root Guru,
Please sit on the lotus and moon seat at my heart.
Please care for me with your great kindness,
And remain firm until I attain the essence of
   enlightenment.

Dedication

Through being cared for throughout all my lives
By Conqueror Tsongkhapa as my Mahayana Guru,
May I never turn away, even for an instant,
From this excellent path praised by the Conquerors.

Inviting Dorje Shugdän and his retinue

HUM
I have the clarity of the Yidam.
Before me in the centre of red and black fire and wind,
On a lotus and sun, trampling demons and obstructors,
Is a terrifying lion, which is powerful and alert.
Upon this sits the great king Dorje Shugdän,
The supreme Heart Jewel of Dharma Protectors.
His body is clothed in the garments of a monk,
And on his head he wears a round, yellow hat.
His hands hold a sword and a heart of compassion.
To his followers he shows an expression of delight,
But to subdue demons and obstructors he displays
    a wrathful manner.
He is surrounded by a vast, assembled retinue,
Such as his attendant Khache Marpo and so forth.

Light rays from my heart instantly invite the wisdom
beings from the sphere of nature, and from all the
different palaces where they abide. They become
inseparable from the commitment beings.

Making offerings and requests

HUM
Respectfully I prostrate with body, speech, and mind.
I offer a mass of inner and outer offerings, blissful tormas,
Alcohol, tea, cakes, milk, and curd,
Both actually set out and mentally imagined, filling the
    whole of space.

Commitment, fulfilling, reliance, and appropriate
    substances,
Outer, inner, secret, attractive, and cleansing offerings,
    filling the whole of space,
I offer these to the entire assembly;
May I fulfil the heart commitment and restore my broken
    commitments.

All my harmful thoughts and actions
That have offended your mind, O Great Protector,
I confess from the depths of my heart.
Please purify them swiftly, and care for me with love, like
a mother for her child.

I beseech you from the depths of my heart, O Supreme
Deity,
Please cause the tradition of Je Tsongkhapa to flourish,
Extend the life and activities of the glorious Gurus,
And increase the study and practice of Dharma within the
Dharma communities.

Please be with me always like the shadow of my body,
And grant me your unwavering care and protection.
Destroy all obstacles and adverse conditions,
Bestow favourable conditions, and fulfil all my wishes.

Now is the time to show clearly your versatile strength
Through your four actions, which are swift, incisive, and
unobstructed,
To fulfil quickly my special heartfelt desires
In accordance with my wishes;

Now is the time to distinguish the truth and falsity of
actions and effects;
Now is the time to dispel false accusations against the
innocent;
Now is the time to protect the pitiful and protectorless;
Now is the time to protect Dharma practitioners as your
children.

In short, from now until I attain the essence of
enlightenment,
I shall honour you as the embodiment of my Guru, Deity,
and Protector.
Therefore please watch over me during the three periods
of the day and the night
And never waver in your actions as my Protector.

Recitation of the mantra

I have the clarity of the Yidam. Before me are the five
lineages of Dorje Shugdän, the great king of Dharma
Protectors. At their hearts are sun cushions upon each of
which there is a HUM surrounded by the mantra rosary
in its appropriate colour. Light rays radiate from the
seed-letter at my heart and touch these. As a result their
minds automatically engage in the pacifying, increasing,
controlling, and wrathful actions that I desire, accomplishing
them without obstruction.

OM VAJRA WIKI WITRANA SÖHA   (21x, 100x, etc.)

OM DHARMAPALA MAHA RADZA VAJRA BEGAWÄN RUDRA:
   PÄNTSA KULA SARWA SHA TRUM MARAYA HUM PHAT
                                (7x, 21x, etc.)

Blessing the tormas

OM KHANDAROHI HUM HUM PHAT
OM SÖBHAWA SHUDDHA SARWA DHARMA SÖBHAWA
   SHUDDHO HAM
Everything become emptiness.

From the state of emptiness, from YAM comes wind, from
RAM comes fire, from AH a grate of three human heads.
Upon this, from AH appears a broad and expansive
skullcup, inside which are the five meats and the five
nectars. These are purified, transformed, and increased
by the three letters, and become a great ocean of
uncontaminated nectar of exalted wisdom.
OM AH HUM   (3x)

Visualizing the guests of the tormas

Before me are the five lineages of Dorje Shugdän, the great
king of Dharma Protectors, together with their retinues.
From HUMs in their tongues come red, single-pronged
vajras. These have straws of light through which they
partake of all the essence of the tormas.

Offering the tormas to the five lineages

OM DHARMAPALA MAHA RADZA VAJRA BEGAWÄN RUDRA:
PÄNTSA KULA SAPARIWARA SARWA BIGNÄN SHA TRUM
IDAM BALINGTA KHA KHA KHAHI KHAHI   (3x)

Offering the tormas to the retinues

OM AHKAROMUKHAM SARWA DHARMANÄN ADENUWATEN
NADÖ DA, NAMA SARWA TATHAGATA AWALOKITE OM
SAMBHARA SAMBHARA HUM   (3x)

Outer offerings

OM DHARMAPALA MAHA RADZA VAJRA BEGAWÄN RUDRA:
PÄNTSA KULA SAPARIWARA AHRGHAM, PADÄM, PUPE,
DHUPE, ALOKE, GÄNDHE, NEWIDE, SHAPTA PARTITZA
HUM SÖHA

Inner offering

OM DHARMAPALA MAHA RADZA VAJRA BEGAWÄN RUDRA:
    PÄNTSA KULA SAPARIWARA OM AH HUM

Special request to Dorje Shugdän

HUM
O Five lineages of Dorje Shugdän together with your
retinues, Protectors of the doctrine of Je Tsongkhapa,
please accept these blissful tormas. Please protect the
doctrine of Buddha, and especially the Sutra and Tantra
teachings of the Protector Manjushri, King of the Dharma,
the great Tsongkhapa. Please increase the renown of the
Three Jewels, protect the community of the Sangha, and
extend the life of the Gurus. For myself, the practitioner,
and all of us disciples, our benefactors, and others, please
dispel all adverse conditions that obstruct the practice of
Dharma. Please establish favourable conditions and
subdue immediately all traitors, enemies, and obstructors
who cause harm and injury, by performing the appropriate
actions swiftly and without delay!

OM DHARMAPALA MAHA RADZA VAJRA BEGAWÄN RUDRA:
PÄNTSA KULA SAPARIWARA DRA GEG AH MU KA MARAYA
PHAT!

Blessing the tsog offering

OM KHANDAROHI HUM HUM PHAT
OM SÖBHAWA SHUDDHA SARWA DHARMA SÖBHAWA
   SHUDDHO HAM
Everything becomes emptiness.

From the state of emptiness, from YAM comes wind, from
RAM comes fire, from AH a grate of three human heads.
Upon this, from AH appears a broad and expansive
skullcup, inside which are the five meats and the five
nectars. These are purified, transformed, and increased
by the three letters, and become a great ocean of
uncontaminated nectar of exalted wisdom.
OM AH HUM   (3x)

Short tsog offering

HUM
I make this tsog offering of uncontaminated enjoyments
To the assembly of Gurus, Yidams, Three Jewels, Dakinis,
   and oath-bound Protectors;
And especially to you, great king Dorje Shugdän,
Supreme Protector of the doctrine of the Gedän tradition,
And to the whole assembly who follow your command.
By your accepting this may the Conqueror Losang's
   tradition
Spread throughout the ten directions.
For all of us disciples, our benefactors, and others,
Please destroy all outer, inner, and secret obstacles.
Please subdue hateful enemies and harmful obstructors,
And swiftly fulfil all our wishes.   (3x)

Tsog offering to the Guru

HO
O Great Hero please listen to me.
Of this we should have no doubt,
Brahmins, dogs, and outcasts are inseparably one.
Considering this, please enjoy this offering.

HO
I am the principal of all the Conquerors,
In actuality the Blessed One Guru Heruka.
I taste this great ocean of wisdom nectar
To satisfy all the Deities.

AH HO MAHA SUKHA

Blessing the golden drink (serkyem)

OM KHANDAROHI HUM HUM PHAT
OM SÖBHAWA SHUDDHA SARWA DHARMA SÖBHAWA
   SHUDDHO HAM
Everything becomes emptiness.

From the state of emptiness, from AH appears a broad and
expansive skullcup. Inside this is the golden drink, which
is the nature of the five meats and the five nectars. This is
purified, transformed, and increased by the three letters,
and becomes a great ocean of uncontaminated nectar of
exalted wisdom.
OM AH HUM   (3x)

Offering the golden drink (serkyem)

HUM
To the Gurus who perform the two purposes and send
   down a rain of excellent blessings,
And to the Yidams who bestow all common and
   uncommon attainments,
I offer this drink of nectar that bestows bliss;
Please partake, and swiftly and spontaneously fulfil all
   my wishes.

To the whole assembly of Heroes and Dakinis of the three
   places,
And to the assembly of powerful, oath-bound Dharma
   Protectors,
I offer this drink of nectar that bestows bliss;
Please partake, and swiftly and spontaneously fulfil all
   my wishes.

Especially to you, supreme, supramundane Protector of
   the doctrine,
Very powerful, swift, and wrathful Dorje Shugdän,
I offer this drink of nectar that bestows bliss;
Please partake, and swiftly and spontaneously fulfil all
   my wishes.

To you, manifestations of the five lineages, who bestow
   without obstruction
Countless pacifying, increasing, controlling, and wrathful
   actions,
I offer this drink of nectar that bestows bliss;
Please partake, and swiftly and spontaneously fulfil all
   my wishes.

To the nine attractive Mothers, the eight guiding Monks,
The ten youthful and wrathful Assistants, and so forth,
I offer this drink of nectar that bestows bliss;
Please partake, and swiftly and spontaneously fulfil all
   my wishes.

To the extremely wrathful Khache Marpo,
The fierce Attendant who opposes those who betray the
   Dharma,
I offer this drink of nectar that bestows bliss;
Please partake, and swiftly and spontaneously fulfil all
   my wishes.

And to all your emanations and their emanations in turn
   who are beyond thought,
The Attendants, gods, and others filling the three
   thousand worlds,

I offer this drink of nectar that bestows bliss;
Please partake, and swiftly and spontaneously fulfil all
my wishes.

Thus, through the power of my making offerings and
requesting your help,
Please perform the four types of action during the six
times;
And always care for me and protect me like a father with
his child,
Without wavering even for a moment.

And may you, the whole assembly of dignified Attendants,
Ever mindful of your solemn oaths to Venerable Düldzin,
Accomplish swiftly and without wavering
Whatever actions I may request of you.

Requesting the fulfilment of wishes

HUM
Whenever your followers with commitments
Request any of the four actions,
Swiftly, incisively, and without delay, you show signs for
all to see;
So please accomplish the actions that I now request of you.

The stainless sun of Je Tsongkhapa's tradition
Shines throughout the sky of samsara and nirvana,
Eliminating the darkness of inferior and wrong paths;
Please cause its light to spread and bring good fortune to
all living beings.

May the glorious Gurus who uphold this tradition
Have indestructible lives, as stable as the supreme victory
banner;
May they send down a rain of deeds fulfilling the wishes
of disciples,
So that Je Tsongkhapa's doctrine will flourish.

Through increasing the study, practice, pure discipline,
and harmony
Of the communities who uphold the stainless doctrine of
Buddha,
And who keep moral discipline with pure minds,
Please cause the Gedän tradition to increase like a waxing
moon.

Through your actions please fulfil the essential wishes
Of all practitioners who uphold the victory banner
Of practising single-pointedly the stages of the paths of
Sutra and Tantra,
The essence of all the teachings they have heard.

Beings throughout this great earth are engaged in
different actions
Of Dharma, non-Dharma, happiness, suffering, cause and
effect;
Through your skilful deeds of preventing and nurturing,
Please lead all beings into the good path to ultimate
happiness.

In particular, please destroy the obstacles and unfavourable
conditions
Of myself and other practitioners.
Increase our lives, our merit, and our resources,
And gather all things animate and inanimate to be freely
enjoyed.

Please be with me always like the shadow of my body,
And care for me always like a friend,
By accomplishing swiftly whatever I wish for,
And whatever I ask of you.

Please perform immediately, without delaying for a year,
or even for a month,
Appropriate actions to eliminate all obstacles
Caused by misguided beings with harmful minds who try
to destroy Je Tsongkhapa's doctrine,
And especially by those who try to harm practitioners.

Please remain in this place always, surrounded by most
   excellent enjoyments.
As my guest, partake continuously of tormas and offerings;
And since you are entrusted with the protection of human
   wealth and enjoyments,
Never waver as my guardian throughout the day and the
   night.

All the attainments I desire
Arise from merely remembering you.
O Wishfulfilling Jewel, Protector of the Dharma,
Please accomplish all my wishes.   (3x)

Giving the remaining tsog offering to the spirits

OM AH HUM   (3x)

HUM
I make this tsog offering of uncontaminated nectar
To the assembly of guests, the regional guardians.
May you enjoy it with delight,
And assist practitioners with your actions.

Dedication

By this virtue may I quickly
Attain the enlightened state of the Guru,
And then lead every living being
Without exception to that ground.

Through my virtues from practising with pure motivation,
May all living beings throughout all their lives
Never be parted from peaceful and wrathful Manjushri,
But always come under their care.

Auspicious prayer

May there be the auspiciousness of the root and lineage
   Gurus,
May there be the auspiciousness of the assembly of Deities
   and Yidams,

May there be the auspiciousness of the Dakas and Dakinis,
And may there be the auspiciousness of the Dharma
  Protectors.

Prayers for the Virtuous Tradition

So that the tradition of Je Tsongkhapa,
The King of the Dharma, may flourish,
May all obstacles be pacified
And may all favourable conditions abound.

Through the two collections of myself and others
Gathered throughout the three times,
May the doctrine of Conqueror Losang Dragpa
Flourish for evermore.

Migtsema prayer

MIG ME TSE WAI TER CHEN CHÄN RÄ ZIG
DRI ME KHYEN PAI WANG PO JAM PÄL YANG
GANG CHÄN KHÄ WAI TSUG GYÄN TSONG KHA PA
LO ZANG DRAG PAI ZHAB LA SÖL WA DEB   (3x)

Colophon: This practice was compiled from traditional sources
by Venerable Geshe Kelsang Gyatso Rinpoche.

Vajradaka Burning Offering

A PRACTICE FOR PURIFYING
MISTAKES AND NEGATIVITIES

by
Ngulchu Dharmabhadra

Vajradaka Burning Offering

Going for refuge

I and all sentient beings, until we achieve enlightenment,
Go for refuge to Buddha, Dharma, and Sangha.   (3x)

Generating bodhichitta

Through the virtues I collect by giving and other
   perfections,
May I become a Buddha for the benefit of all.   (3x)

Generating special bodhichitta

And especially for the sake of all mother sentient beings,
I must attain the state of complete Buddhahood as quickly
as possible. Therefore I shall engage in a burning offering
to Vajradaka.

Visualizing the commitment being

OM VAJRA AMRITA KUNDALI HANA HANA HUM PHAT
OM SÖBHAWA SHUDDHA SARWA DHARMA SÖBHAWA
   SHUDDHO HAM
The fire becomes emptiness.

From the state of emptiness there arises a fiercely blazing
fire of exalted wisdom. In the centre of this, from a HUM
and a vajra, there arises wrathful Vajradaka, dark blue in
colour. He has one face and two hands, which are joined in
the mudra of a Hungdzä and hold a vajra and bell. With
his mouth wide open, he snarls into space, baring his four
sharp fangs. His head is adorned with five dry skulls and

he wears a long necklace of fifty moist skulls. He wears a tiger's skin for a lower garment and is complete with all the features of a wrathful manifestation. He sits with his legs forming a circle, in the manner of a Hero destroying negativities and obstructions. At his crown is a white OM, at his throat a red AH, at his heart a blue HUM.

Inviting and absorbing the wisdom beings

Light rays radiate from the HUM at his heart and invite from their natural abodes wisdom beings in the same aspect, together with the empowering Deities.

DZA HUM BAM HO
They become non-dual.

Granting empowerment

The empowering Deities grant empowerment and his crown is adorned by Akshobya.

Offerings

OM VAJRADAKA SAPARIWARA AHRGHAM PARTITZA HUM SÖHA
OM VAJRADAKA SAPARIWARA PADÄM PARTITZA HUM SÖHA
OM VAJRADAKA SAPARIWARA PUPE PARTITZA HUM SÖHA
OM VAJRADAKA SAPARIWARA DHUPE PARTITZA HUM SÖHA
OM VAJRADAKA SAPARIWARA ALOKE PARTITZA HUM SÖHA
OM VAJRADAKA SAPARIWARA GÄNDHE PARTITZA HUM SÖHA
OM VAJRADAKA SAPARIWARA NEWIDE PARTITZA HUM SÖHA
OM VAJRADAKA SAPARIWARA SHAPTA PARTITZA HUM SÖHA

Prostration

O Vajra Akshobya, great exalted wisdom,
Great skilful one from the vajra sphere,
Supreme among the three vajras and three mandalas,
To you Vajradaka I prostrate.

Visualization for making the burning offering

I remain in my ordinary form. At my heart is a black letter PAM, the seed of negativity. At my navel, from RAM, comes a red fire mandala. On the soles of both my feet, from YAM, comes a blue wind mandala.

Light rays radiate from the letter PAM and draw back all the negativities and obstructions of my three doors in the aspect of black rays of light. These dissolve into the PAM.

Below, the wind blows and enters through the soles of my feet. The fire at my navel blazes and light rays from the fire drive the PAM out through my nostrils. My negativities take on the aspect of a scorpion, which dissolves into the sesame seeds. I offer these to the mouth of Vajradaka.

OM VAJRA DAKA KHA KHA KHAHI KHAHI SARWA PAPAM
DAHANA BHAKMI KURU SÖHA

May all the negativities, obstructions, and degenerated commitments I have accumulated during beginningless lives in samsara [be purified] SHÄNTING KURUYE SÖHA

Offer the sesame seeds to Vajradaka while reciting the mantra and the brief request prayer. Continue in this way until all the sesame seeds have been offered.

Thanking offering

OM VAJRADAKA SAPARIWARA AHRGHAM, PADÄM, PUPE,
DHUPE, ALOKE, GÄNDHE, NEWIDE, SHAPTA PARTITZA
HUM SÖHA

Prostration

Merely by our remembering your dark-blue form of
 a wrathful cannibal,
Amidst a blazing mass of exalted wisdom fire,
You destroy all maras, negativities, and obstructions;
To you Vajradaka I prostrate.

159

Requesting forbearance

Whatever mistakes I have made
Through not finding, not understanding,
Or not having the ability,
Please, O Protector, be patient with all of these.

Dissolution

The wisdom beings return to their natural abodes, and
the commitment being transforms into the aspect of a
blazing fire.

Dedication

By this virtue, throughout all my lives
May I never be parted from the Mahayana Guru who
    reveals the unmistaken path,
And by always remaining under his care
May I drink continuously from the nectar of his speech.

Due to this, may I and others complete the practices
Of renunciation, bodhichitta, correct view,
The six perfections, and the two stages,
And may we swiftly attain the state endowed with the ten
    powers.

Through the blessings of the non-deceptive Guru and
    Three Jewels,
And the power of the immutable nature of phenomena
    and non-deceptive dependent relationship,
May everything be auspicious for my excellent prayers to
    be accomplished
So that I may swiftly attain omniscient Buddhahood.

Colophon: This sadhana was translated under the compassionate
guidance of Venerable Geshe Kelsang Gyatso.

Glossary

Akshobya The manifestation of the aggregate of consciousness of all Buddhas. He has a blue-coloured body.

Amitabha The manifestation of the aggregate of discrimination of all Buddhas. He has a red-coloured body.

Atisha (AD 982-1054) A famous Indian Buddhist scholar and meditation master. He was Abbot of the great Buddhist monastery of Vikramashila at a time when Mahayana Buddhism was flourishing in India. He was later invited to Tibet and his arrival there led to the re-establishment of Buddhism in Tibet. He is the author of the first text on the stages of the path, *Lamp for the Path*. His tradition later became known as the 'Kadampa Tradition'. See *Joyful Path of Good Fortune*.

Attainments (Skt. siddhi) These are of two types: common attainments and supreme attainments. Common attainments are of four principal types: pacifying attainments, increasing attainments, controlling attainments, and wrathful attainments. Supreme attainments are the special realizations of a Buddha. See *Tantric Grounds and Paths*.

Basis of imputation All phenomena are imputed upon their parts, therefore any of the individual parts, or the entire collection of the parts, of any phenomenon is its basis of imputation. A phenomenon is imputed by mind in dependence upon its basis of imputation appearing to that mind. See *Heart of Wisdom* and *Ocean of Nectar*.

Blessing (Tib. jin gyi lab pa) The transformation of our mind from a negative state to a positive state, from an unhappy state to a happy state, or from a state of weakness to a state of strength, through the inspiration of holy beings such as our Spiritual Guide, Buddhas, and Bodhisattvas.

Bodhichitta Sanskrit word for 'mind of enlightenment'. 'Bodhi' means 'enlightenment', and 'chitta' means 'mind'. There are two types of bodhichitta – conventional bodhichitta and ultimate bodhichitta. Generally speaking, the term 'bodhichitta' refers to conventional bodhichitta, which is a primary mind motivated by great

161

compassion that spontaneously seeks enlightenment to benefit all living beings. There are two types of conventional bodhichitta – aspiring bodhichitta and engaging bodhichitta. Ultimate bodhichitta is a wisdom motivated by conventional bodhichitta that directly realizes emptiness, the ultimate nature of phenomena. See *Joyful Path of Good Fortune* and *Meaningful to Behold*.

Bodhisattva A person who has generated spontaneous bodhichitta but who has not yet become a Buddha. See *Joyful Path of Good Fortune* and *Meaningful to Behold*.

Body mandala The transformation into a Deity of any part of the body of a self-generated or in-front-generated Deity. See *Guide to Dakini Land*, *Great Treasury of Merit*, and *Essence of Vajrayana*.

Brahma A worldly god (Skt. deva). See *Ocean of Nectar*.

Buddha A being who has completely abandoned all delusions and their imprints. See *Joyful Path of Good Fortune*.

Buddha family There are five main Buddha families: the families of Vairochana, Ratnasambhava, Amitabha, Amoghasiddhi, and Akshobya. They are the five purified aggregates – the aggregates of form, feeling, discrimination, compositional factors, and consciousness, respectively; and the five exalted wisdoms – the exalted mirror-like wisdom, the exalted wisdom of equality, the exalted wisdom of individual realization, the exalted wisdom of accomplishing activities, and the exalted wisdom of the Dharmadhatu, respectively. See *Great Treasury of Merit*.

Buddha Shakyamuni The fourth of one thousand Buddhas who are to appear in this world during this Fortunate Aeon. The first three were Krakuchchanda, Kanakamuni, and Kashyapa. The fifth Buddha will be Maitreya. See *Introduction to Buddhism*.

Central channel The principal channel at the very centre of the body along which the channel wheels are located. See *Clear Light of Bliss*.

Chakra See *Channel wheel*.

Channel wheel (Skt. chakra) A focal centre where secondary channels branch out from the central channel. Meditating on these points can cause the inner winds to enter the central channel. See *Clear Light of Bliss*.

Clear appearance Generally, any clear appearance of an object of meditation to the concentration focused on it. More specifically, a Secret Mantra practice whereby the practitioner, having generated himself or herself as a Deity and the environment as the Deity's mandala, tries to attain clear appearance of the whole object to his or her concentration. It is the antidote to ordinary appearance. See *Guide to Dakini Land*.

Clear light A manifest very subtle mind that perceives an appearance like clear, empty space. See *Clear Light of Bliss*.

Close retreat A retreat during which we strive to draw close to a particular Deity. This can be understood in two ways: drawing close in the sense of developing a special relationship with a friend, and drawing close in the sense of becoming more and more like the Deity. An action close retreat is a close retreat in which we collect a certain number of mantras and conclude with a fire puja. See *Guide to Dakini Land* and *Tantric Grounds and Paths*.

Collection of merit A virtuous action motivated by bodhichitta that is a main cause of attaining the Form Body of a Buddha. Examples are making offerings and prostrations to holy beings with bodhichitta motivation, and the practice of the perfections of giving, moral discipline, and patience.

Collection of wisdom A virtuous mental action motivated by bodhichitta that is a main cause of attaining the Truth Body of a Buddha. Examples are listening to, contemplating, and meditating on emptiness with bodhichitta motivation.

Commitment being A visualized Buddha or ourself visualized as a Buddha. A commitment being is so called because in general it is the commitment of all Buddhists to visualize or remember Buddha, and in particular it is a commitment of those who have received an empowerment into Highest Yoga Tantra to generate themselves as a Deity.

Compassion A mind that cannot bear the suffering of others and wishes them to be free from it. See also *Great compassion*. See *Joyful Path of Good Fortune*.

Completion stage Highest Yoga Tantra realizations developed in dependence upon the winds entering, abiding, and dissolving within the central channel through the force of meditation. See *Clear Light of Bliss*, *Tantric Grounds and Paths*, *Guide to Dakini Land*, and *Essence of Vajrayana*.

Concentration being A symbol of Buddha's Truth Body, usually visualized as a seed-letter at the heart of a commitment being or a wisdom being. It is so called because it is generated through concentration.

Contaminated aggregate Any of the aggregates of form, feeling, discrimination, compositional factors, and consciousness of a samsaric being. See *Heart of Wisdom*.

Conventional truth Any phenomenon other than emptiness. Conventional truths are true with respect to the minds of ordinary beings, but in reality they are false. See *Heart of Wisdom*, *Meaningful to Behold*, and *Ocean of Nectar*.

Degenerate times A period when spiritual activity degenerates.

Deity (Skt. Yidam) A Tantric enlightened being.

Demon (Skt. mara) Anything that obstructs the attainment of liberation or enlightenment. There are four principal types of demon: the demon of the delusions, the demon of contaminated aggregates, the demon of uncontrolled death, and the Devaputra demons. Of these, only the last are actual sentient beings. See *Heart of Wisdom* and *Ocean of Nectar*.

Desire realm The environment of hell beings, hungry ghosts, animals, humans, demi-gods, and the gods who enjoy the five objects of desire.

Dharmakaya Sanskrit word for the Truth Body of a Buddha.

Dharmakirti A great Indian Buddhist Yogi and scholar who composed *Commentary to Valid Cognition*, a commentary to *Compendium of Valid Cognition*, which was written by his Spiritual Guide, Dignaga. See *Understanding the Mind*.

Divine pride A non-deluded pride that regards oneself as a Deity and one's environment and enjoyments as those of the Deity. It is the antidote to ordinary conceptions. See *Guide to Dakini Land*.

Dualistic appearance The appearance to mind of an object together with the inherent existence of that object. See *Heart of Wisdom*.

Emanation Body (Skt. Nirmanakaya) A Buddha's Form Body that can be perceived by ordinary beings. See *Tantric Grounds and Paths*.

Empowerment A special potential power to attain any of the four Buddha bodies that is received by a Tantric practitioner from his or her Guru, or from other holy beings, by means of Tantric ritual. It is the gateway to the Vajrayana.

Emptiness Lack of inherent existence, the ultimate nature of phenomena. See *Heart of Wisdom* and *Ocean of Nectar*.

Enjoyment Body (Skt. Sambhogakaya) A Buddha's subtle Form Body that can be perceived only by Mahayana Superiors. See *Tantric Grounds and Paths*.

Exalted awareness A spiritual realization that knows perfectly the nature of its principal object. Sometimes called 'exalted wisdom'. See *Tantric Grounds and Paths*.

Exalted wisdom See *Exalted awareness*.

Field for Accumulating Merit The Three Jewels. Just as external seeds grow in a field of soil, so the virtuous internal seeds produced by virtuous actions grow in dependence upon Buddha Jewel, Dharma Jewel, and Sangha Jewel. Also known as 'Field of Merit'.

Foe Destroyer (Skt. Arhat) A practitioner who has abandoned all delusions and their seeds by training on the spiritual paths, and who will never again be born in samsara. In this context the term 'Foe' refers to the delusions.

Fortunate Aeon The name given to this world age. It is so called because one thousand Buddhas will appear during this aeon. Buddha Shakyamuni was the fourth and Buddha Maitreya will be the fifth. An aeon in which no Buddhas appear is called a 'Dark Aeon'.

Four fearlessnesses Special qualities of a Buddha. A fearlessness is an utterly firm, ultimate realization that is entirely free from fear in expounding Dharma. See *Tantric Grounds and Paths* and *Ocean of Nectar*.

Four maras See *Demon*.

Four noble truths True sufferings, true origins, true cessations, and true paths. They are called 'noble' truths because they are supreme objects of meditation. Through meditation on these four objects we can realize ultimate truth directly and thus become a noble, or Superior, being. Sometimes referred to as the 'four truths of Superiors'. See *Joyful Path of Good Fortune*.

Generation stage A realization of a creative yoga prior to attaining the actual completion stage, attained as a result of the pure concentration on bringing the three bodies into the path in which one mentally generates oneself as a Tantric Deity and one's surroundings as the Deity's mandala. Meditation on generation stage is called a 'creative yoga' because its object is created by correct imagination. See *Tantric Grounds and Paths*, *Guide to Dakini Land*, and *Essence of Vajrayana*.

Generic image The appearing object of a conceptual mind. The conceptual mind mistakes the generic image for the object itself. For example, if we think about our mother, an image of our mother appears to our conceptual mind, and it seems to that mind as if our mother herself is appearing. However, the object that principally appears to that mind is the generic image of our mother. This generic image appears to our mind through the mental exclusion of all objects that are not our mother. It is therefore the appearance of a non-non-mother. See *Understanding the Mind*.

Great compassion A mind wishing to protect all sentient beings from suffering. See *Ocean of Nectar*.

Heruka A principal Deity of Mother Tantra who is the embodiment of indivisible bliss and emptiness. He has a blue-coloured body, four faces, and twelve arms, and embraces his consort Vajravarahi. See *Essence of Vajrayana*.

Highest Yoga Tantra A Tantric instruction that includes the method for transforming sexual bliss into the spiritual path. See *Tantric Grounds and Paths*.

Hinayana Sanskrit word for 'Lesser Vehicle'. The Hinayana goal is to attain merely one's own liberation from suffering by completely abandoning delusions. See *Joyful Path of Good Fortune*.

Ignorance A mental factor that is confused about the ultimate nature of phenomena. See *Understanding the Mind*.

Illusory body When a practitioner of Highest Yoga Tantra rises from the meditation of the isolated mind of ultimate example clear light he or she attains a body that is not the same as his or her ordinary physical body. This new body is the illusory body. It has the same appearance as the body of the personal Deity of generation stage except that it is white in colour, and it can be perceived only by those who have already attained an illusory body. See *Tantric Grounds and Paths* and *Clear Light of Bliss*.

Indra A worldly god (Skt. deva). See *Heart of Wisdom*.

Inherent existence An imagined mode of existence whereby phenomena are held to exist from their own side, independent of other phenomena. In reality all phenomena are empty of inherent existence because they depend upon their parts. See *Heart of Wisdom* and *Ocean of Nectar*.

Kalarupa A Dharma Protector who is an emanation of Manjushri.

Kangyur The collection of all the Sutras and Tantras that have been translated from Sanskrit into Tibetan. See also *Tängyur*.

Lamrim Literally, 'stages of the path'. A special arrangement of all Buddha's teachings that is easy to understand and put into practice. It reveals all the stages of the path to enlightenment. See *Joyful Path of Good Fortune* and *The Meditation Handbook*.

Liberation Complete freedom from samsara and its cause, the delusions. See *Joyful Path of Good Fortune*.

Lineage A line of instruction that has been passed down from Teacher to disciple, with each Guru in the line having gained personal experience of the instruction before passing it on to others.

Lojong See *Training the mind*.

Losang Dragpa (Skt. Sumati Kirti) The ordained name of Je Tsongkhapa. See *Great Treasury of Merit*.

Madhyamika The higher of the two schools of Mahayana tenets. The Madhyamika view was taught by Buddha in the *Perfection of Wisdom Sutras* during the second turning of the Wheel of Dharma and was subsequently elucidated by Nagarjuna and his followers. There are two divisions of this school, Madhyamika-Svatantrika and Madhyamika-Prasangika, of which the latter is Buddha's final view. See *Meaningful to Behold* and *Ocean of Nectar*.

Mahakala A Dharma Protector who appears in many different aspects – four-armed, six-armed, four-faced, etc.

Mahamudra Literally, 'great seal'. According to Sutra this refers to the profound view of emptiness. Since emptiness is the nature of all phenomena it is called a 'seal', and since a direct realization of emptiness enables us to accomplish the great purpose – complete liberation from the sufferings of samsara – it is also called 'great'. According to Secret Mantra, great seal is the union of spontaneous great bliss and emptiness. See *Clear Light of Bliss*.

Mahasiddha Sanskrit word for 'greatly accomplished one'. Used to refer to Yogis or Yoginis with high attainments.

Mahayana Sanskrit word for 'Great Vehicle', the spiritual path to great enlightenment. The Mahayana goal is to attain Buddhahood for the benefit of all sentient beings by completely abandoning delusions and their imprints. See *Joyful Path of Good Fortune*.

Maitreya The embodiment of the loving-kindness of all the Buddhas. At the time of Buddha Shakyamuni he manifested as a Bodhisattva disciple. In the future he will manifest as the fifth universal Buddha.

Mandala offering An offering of the entire universe visualized as a Pure Land with all the inhabitants as pure beings. See *Guide to Dakini Land*.

Manjushri The embodiment of the wisdom of all the Buddhas. At the time of Buddha Shakyamuni he manifested as a Bodhisattva disciple. See *Great Treasury of Merit*.

Mantra Literally, 'mind protection'. Mantra protects the mind from ordinary appearances and conceptions. See *Guide to Dakini Land* and *Tantric Grounds and Paths*.

Mara See *Demon*.

Meditative equipoise Single-pointed concentration on a virtuous object such as emptiness. See *Ocean of Nectar*.

Merit The good fortune created by virtuous actions. It is the potential power to increase our good qualities and produce happiness.

Moral discipline A virtuous mental determination to abandon any fault, or a bodily or verbal action motivated by such a determination. See *Joyful Path of Good Fortune*.

Mount Meru According to Buddhist cosmology, a divine mountain that stands at the centre of the universe.

Nalanda Monastery A great seat of Buddhist learning and practice in ancient India.

Non-virtuous actions The ten non-virtuous actions are: killing, stealing, sexual misconduct, lying, divisive speech, hurtful speech, idle gossip, covetousness, malice, and holding wrong views. See *Joyful Path of Good Fortune*.

Obstructions to liberation Obstructions that prevent the attainment of liberation. All delusions, such as ignorance, attachment, and anger, together with their seeds, are obstructions to liberation. Also called 'delusion-obstructions'.

Obstructions to omniscience The imprints of delusions that prevent simultaneous and direct realization of all phenomena. Only Buddhas have overcome these obstructions.

Offering to the Spiritual Guide (Tib. *Lama Chöpa*) A special Guru yoga of Je Tsongkhapa in which our Spiritual Guide is visualized in the aspect of Lama Losang Tubwang Dorjechang. The instruction for this practice was revealed by Buddha Manjushri in the *Kadam Emanation Scripture* and written down by the first Panchen Lama.

It is an essential preliminary practice for Vajrayana Mahamudra. See *Great Treasury of Merit*.

Ordinary appearance Any appearance that is due to an impure mind. According to the teachings of Secret Mantra, ordinary appearance is the main cause of samsara. See *Tantric Grounds and Paths*.

Ordinary conception Any mind that conceives things as ordinary. See *Tantric Grounds and Paths*.

Perfection of Wisdom Sutras Sutras of the second turning of the Wheel of Dharma in which Buddha revealed his final view of the ultimate nature of all phenomena – emptiness of inherent existence. See *Heart of Wisdom* and *Ocean of Nectar*.

Pratimoksha Sanskrit word for 'individual liberation'. See *The Bodhisattva Vow*.

Profound path The profound path includes all the wisdom practices that lead to a direct realization of emptiness and ultimately to the Truth Body of a Buddha. See *Joyful Path of Good Fortune* and *Ocean of Nectar*.

Puja A ceremony in which offerings and other acts of devotion are performed in front of holy beings.

Pure Land A pure environment in which there are no true sufferings. There are many Pure Lands. For example, Tushita is the Pure Land of Buddha Maitreya; Sukhavati is the Pure Land of Buddha Amitabha; and Dakini Land, or Keajra, is the Pure Land of Buddha Vajrayogini. See *Guide to Dakini Land*.

Renunciation The wish to be released from samsara. See *Joyful Path of Good Fortune*.

Root Guru The main Spiritual Guide from whom we have received the empowerments, instructions, and oral transmissions of our main practice. See *Great Treasury of Merit*.

Sadhana A ritual that is a method for developing spiritual realizations. It can be associated with either Sutra or Tantra.

Samsara The cycle of uncontrolled death and rebirth, or the cycle of twelve dependent-related links. See *Joyful Path of Good Fortune*.

Sangha According to the Vinaya tradition, any community of four or more fully ordained monks or nuns. In general, ordained or lay people who take Bodhisattva vows or Tantric vows can also be said to be Sangha.

Secret Mantra Synonymous with Tantra. Secret Mantra teachings are distinguished from Sutra teachings in that they reveal methods for training the mind by bringing the future result, or Buddhahood, into the present path. Secret Mantra is the supreme path to full enlightenment. See *Tantric Grounds and Paths* and *Clear Light of Bliss*.

Seed-letter The sacred letter from which a Deity is generated. Each Deity has a particular seed-letter. For example, the seed-letter of Manjushri is DHI, of Tara is TAM, of Vajrayogini is BAM, and of Heruka is HUM.

Self-cherishing A mental attitude that considers oneself to be precious or important. It is regarded as a principal object to be abandoned by Bodhisattvas. See *Universal Compassion*.

Self-grasping A conceptual mind that grasps any phenomenon to be inherently existent. The mind of self-grasping gives rise to all other delusions such as anger and attachment. It is the root cause of all suffering and dissatisfaction. See *Joyful Path of Good Fortune*.

Six perfections The perfections of giving, moral discipline, patience, effort, mental stabilization, and wisdom. They are called 'perfections' because they are motivated by bodhichitta. See *Joyful Path of Good Fortune*, *Meaningful to Behold*, *The Bodhisattva Vow*, and *Ocean of Nectar*.

Stages of the path See *Lamrim*.

Superior being (Skt. Arya) A being who has a direct realization of emptiness. There are Hinayana Superiors and Mahayana Superiors.

Superior seeing A special wisdom that sees its object clearly, and that is maintained by tranquil abiding and the special suppleness that is induced by investigation. See *Joyful Path of Good Fortune*.

Supreme Emanation Body A special Emanation Body displaying the thirty-two major signs and eighty minor indications that can be seen by ordinary beings only if they have very pure karma. See also *Emanation Body*.

Sutra The teachings of Buddha that are open to everyone to practise without the need for empowerment. These include Buddha's teachings of the three turnings of the Wheel of Dharma.

Tängyur The collection of commentaries to Buddha's teachings that have been translated from Sanskrit into Tibetan. See also *Kangyur*.

Ten directions The four cardinal directions, the four intermediate directions, and the directions above and below.

Thirty-two major signs Sometimes called the 'major marks'. Special characteristics of a Buddha's form. Examples are the sign of the wheel on the palms of the hands and the soles of the feet. The eighty indications, sometimes called the 'minor marks', include signs such as copper-coloured nails.

Torma offering A special food offering made according to either Sutric or Tantric rituals. See *Guide to Dakini Land* and *Essence of Vajrayana*.

Training the mind (Tib. Lojong) A special lineage of instructions deriving from Manjushri and passed down through Shantideva, Atisha, and the Kadampa Geshes, that emphasizes the generation of bodhichitta through the practices of equalizing and exchanging self with others combined with taking and giving. See *Universal Compassion*.

Tranquil abiding A concentration that possesses the special bliss of physical and mental suppleness that is attained in dependence upon completing the nine mental abidings. See *Joyful Path of Good Fortune* and *Meaningful to Behold*.

Transference of consciousness (Tib. powa) A practice for transferring the consciousness to a Pure Land at the time of death. See *Great Treasury of Merit*.

True cessation The ultimate nature of a mind freed from any obstruction by means of a true path. See *Joyful Path of Good Fortune*.

True origin An action or a delusion that is the main cause of a true suffering. See *Joyful Path of Good Fortune*.

True path A spiritual path held by a wisdom directly realizing emptiness. See *Joyful Path of Good Fortune*.

True suffering A contaminated object produced by delusions and karma. See *Joyful Path of Good Fortune*.

Tsog offering An offering made by an assembly of Heroes and Heroines. See *Guide to Dakini Land* and *Great Treasury of Merit*.

Ultimate truth The ultimate nature of all phenomena, emptiness. See *Heart of Wisdom*, *Meaningful to Behold*, and *Ocean of Nectar*.

Uncontaminated bliss A realization of bliss conjoined with a wisdom directly realizing emptiness. See *Guide to Dakini Land* and *Tantric Grounds and Paths*.

Union of No More Learning A union of the pure illusory body and meaning clear light that has abandoned the obstructions to omniscience. Synonymous with Buddhahood. See *Clear Light of Bliss* and *Tantric Grounds and Paths*.

Union that needs learning A union of the pure illusory body and meaning clear light that has not yet abandoned the obstructions to omniscience. See *Clear Light of Bliss* and *Tantric Grounds and Paths*.

Vajra body Generally, the channels, drops, and inner winds. More specifically, the pure illusory body. The body of a Buddha is known as the 'resultant vajra body'. See *Clear Light of Bliss*.

Vajradaka burning offering A special purification practice in which our negativities and downfalls are transformed into black sesame seeds, which are then offered to Vajradaka who appears from a blazing fire to consume them. See *Guide to Dakini Land*.

Vajradhara The founder of Vajrayana. He is the same mental continuum as Buddha Shakyamuni but displays a different aspect. Buddha Shakyamuni appears in the aspect of an Emanation Body and Conqueror Vajradhara appears in the aspect of an Enjoyment Body. See *Great Treasury of Merit*.

Vajrapani The embodiment of the power of all the Buddhas. He appears in a wrathful aspect, displaying his power to overcome outer, inner, and secret obstacles. At the time of Buddha Shakyamuni he manifested as a Bodhisattva disciple.

Vajra posture The perfect cross-legged posture. See *Meaningful to Behold*.

Vajrayana The Secret Mantra vehicle. See *Tantric Grounds and Paths*.

Vajrayogini A female Highest Yoga Tantra Deity who is the embodiment of indivisible bliss and emptiness. She is the same nature as Heruka. See *Guide to Dakini Land*.

Vast path The vast path includes all the method practices from the initial cultivation of compassion through to the final attainment of the Form Body of a Buddha. See *Joyful Path of Good Fortune* and *Ocean of Nectar*.

Vinaya Sutras Sutras in which Buddha principally explains the practice of moral discipline, and in particular the Pratimoksha moral discipline.

Vows Promises to refrain from certain actions. The three sets of vows are the Pratimoksha vows of individual liberation, the Bodhisattva vows, and the Secret Mantra vows. See *The Bodhisattva Vow* and *Tantric Grounds and Paths*.

Wheel of Dharma Buddha gave his teachings in three main phases, which are known as 'the three turnings of the Wheel of Dharma'. During the first Wheel he taught the four noble truths, during the second he taught the *Perfection of Wisdom Sutras* and revealed the view of the Madhyamika-Prasangika, and during the third he taught the Chittamatra view. See *Ocean of Nectar*.

Wisdom A virtuous, intelligent mind that makes its primary mind realize its object thoroughly. A wisdom is a spiritual path that functions to release our mind from delusions or their imprints. An example of wisdom is the correct view of emptiness. See *Understanding the Mind*.

Wisdom being An actual Buddha, especially one who is invited to unite with a visualized commitment being.

Yamantaka A Highest Yoga Tantra Deity who is a wrathful manifestation of Manjushri.

Yidam See *Deity*.

Bibliography

Geshe Kelsang Gyatso is a highly respected meditation master and scholar of the Mahayana Buddhist tradition founded by Je Tsongkhapa. Since arriving in the UK in 1977, Geshe Kelsang has worked tirelessly to establish pure Buddhadharma throughout the world. Over this period he has given extensive teachings on the major scriptures of the Mahayana. These teachings are currently being published and provide a comprehensive presentation of the essential Sutra and Tantra practices of Mahayana Buddhism.

Books in print

The Bodhisattva Vow. The essential practices of Mahayana Buddhism. (2nd. edn. Tharpa, 1995.)

Buddhism in the Tibetan Tradition. A guide to Tibetan Buddhism. (2nd. edn. Penguin, 1990.)

Clear Light of Bliss. The practice of Mahamudra in Vajrayana Buddhism. (2nd. edn. Tharpa, 1992.)

Great Treasury of Merit. The practice of relying upon a Spiritual Guide. (Tharpa, 1992.)

Guide to Dakini Land. The Highest Yoga Tantra practice of Buddha Vajrayogini. (2nd. edn. Tharpa, 1996.)

Heart Jewel. The essential practices of Kadampa Buddhism. (2nd. edn. Tharpa, 1997.)

Heart of Wisdom. The essential wisdom teachings of Buddha. (3rd. edn. Tharpa, 1996.)

Introduction to Buddhism. An explanation of the Buddhist way of life. (Rev. 1st. edn. Tharpa, 1995.)

Joyful Path of Good Fortune. The Buddhist path to enlightenment. (2nd. edn. Tharpa, 1996.)

Meaningful to Behold. The Bodhisattva's way of life. (4th. edn. Tharpa, 1994.)

The Meditation Handbook. A practical guide to Buddhist meditation. (3rd. edn. Tharpa, 1995.)

Ocean of Nectar. Wisdom and compassion in Mahayana Buddhism. (Tharpa, 1995.)

Tantric Grounds and Paths. How to enter, progress on, and
complete the Vajrayana path. (Tharpa, 1994.)
Understanding the Mind. An explanation of the nature and functions
of the mind. (Tharpa, 1993.)
Universal Compassion. Transforming your life through love and
compassion. (3rd. edn. Tharpa, 1997.)

Sadhanas

Geshe Kelsang has also supervised the translation of a collection of
essential sadhanas, or prayer booklets. Those in print include:

Assembly of Good Fortune. The tsog offering for Heruka body
mandala.
Avalokiteshvara Sadhana. Prayers and requests to the Buddha of
compassion.
The Bodhisattva's Confession of Moral Downfalls. The purification
practice of the *Mahayana Sutra of the Three Superior Heaps.*
Condensed Essence of Vajrayana. Condensed Heruka body mandala
self-generation sadhana.
Dakini Yoga: Vajrayogini Six-Session Sadhana. Six-session Guru yoga
combined with self-generation as Vajrayogini.
Drop of Essential Nectar. A special fasting and purification practice
in conjunction with Eleven-faced Avalokiteshvara.
Essence of Good Fortune. Prayers for the six preparatory practices
for meditation on the stages of the path to enlightenment.
Essence of Vajrayana (1). The condensed meaning of Vajrayana
Mahamudra and prayers of request to the lineage Gurus.
Essence of Vajrayana (2). Heruka body mandala self-generation
sadhana according to the system of Mahasiddha Ghantapa.
Feast of Great Bliss. Vajrayogini self-initiation sadhana.
Great Compassionate Mother. The sadhana of Arya Tara.
Great Liberation of the Father. Preliminary prayers for Mahamudra
meditation in conjunction with Heruka practice.
Great Liberation of the Mother. Preliminary prayers for Mahamudra
meditation in conjunction with Vajrayogini practice.
The Great Mother. A method to overcome hindrances and obstacles
by reciting the *Essence of Wisdom Sutra* (the *Heart Sutra*).
Heart Jewel. The Guru yoga of Je Tsongkhapa combined with the
condensed sadhana of his Dharma Protector.
The Hundreds of Deities of the Joyful Land. The Guru yoga of Je
Tsongkhapa.
The Kadampa Way of Life. Essential practices of the New Kadampa
Tradition.
Liberation from Sorrow. Praises and requests to the Twenty-one Taras.

Medicine Guru Sadhana. The method for making requests to the Assembly of Seven Medicine Buddhas.

Meditation and Recitation of Solitary Vajrasattva.

Melodious Drum Victorious in all Directions. The extensive fulfilling and restoring ritual of the Dharma Protector, the great king Dorje Shugdän, in conjunction with Mahakala, Kalarupa, Kalindewi, and other Dharma Protectors.

Offering to the Spiritual Guide (Lama Chöpa). A special Guru yoga practice of Je Tsongkhapa's tradition.

Prayers for Meditation. Brief preparatory prayers for meditation.

A Pure Life. The practice of taking and keeping the eight Mahayana precepts.

The Quick Path. A condensed practice of Heruka Five Deities according to Master Ghantapa's tradition.

Treasury of Wisdom. The sadhana of Venerable Manjushri.

Quick Path to Great Bliss. Vajrayogini self-generation sadhana.

Wishfulfilling Jewel. The Guru yoga of Je Tsongkhapa combined with the sadhana of his Dharma Protector.

The Yoga of Buddha Amitayus. A special method for increasing life span, wisdom, and merit.

For a catalogue of all our publications please contact:

Tharpa Publications
Kilnwick Percy Hall
Pocklington
York YO4 2UF
England

Tel: 01759-306446
Fax: 01759-306397

E-mail: tharpa@rmplc.co.uk
Website: http://www.luna.co.uk/~tharpa

- NKT -

Study Programmes

Geshe Kelsang has prepared three study programmes based on his books: the General Programme, the Foundation Programme, and the Teacher Training Programme. These are designed to fulfil the wishes of those who would like to study Buddhism systematically and thereby deepen their experience of the essential practices.

The **General Programme** provides a basic introduction to Buddhist view, meditation, and action, and various kinds of teaching and practice from both Sutra and Tantra.

The **Foundation Programme** is designed for those who prefer a more structured approach to their spiritual training. Based on five of Geshe Kelsang's books, this programme lasts for approximately four years. The classes consist of readings, teachings, discussion, pujas, and meditations. Each subject concludes with an examination.

The **Teacher Training Programme** is designed for those who wish to train as authentic Dharma Teachers. This programme, which takes approximately seven years to complete, is based on twelve of Geshe Kelsang's books. To qualify as Dharma Teachers, participants must complete the study of all twelve texts, pass an examination in each subject, satisfy certain criteria with regard to behaviour and life style, and complete various meditation retreats.

These three programmes are taught worldwide at Centres of the New Kadampa Tradition. All these Centres are under the spiritual direction of Geshe Kelsang. The three main Centres are:

Manjushri Centre, Conishead Priory, Ulverston, Cumbria, LA12 9QQ, UK. Tel: 01229-584029. manjushri@tcp.co.uk. Founded 1975.

Madhyamaka Centre, Kilnwick Percy Hall, Pocklington, York, YO4 2UF, UK. Tel: 01759-304832. madhyama@rmplc.co.uk. Founded 1979.

Vajradakini Buddhist Center, 1024 Murl Drive, Irving, Texas 75062-4440, USA. Tel/Fax: 214-570-3091.

Addresses of all the other Centres are available from: James Belither, Secretary, the New Kadampa Tradition (NKT), Conishead Priory, Ulverston, Cumbria, LA12 9QQ, UK. Tel: 01229-584029. kadampa@dircon.co.uk.

Index

The letter 'g' indicates an entry in the glossary.

actions of immediate retribution 77-8
aggregates 90
  contaminated 61, g
Ajatashatru, King 77
Akshobya, Buddha 51, g
Altan Khan 86
Amitabha, Buddha 51, g
Ashoka 29
Atisha 20, 90, g
attainments g
  common 95
  of a Tantric Deity 53-5
  receiving 31
  sign of 55
  supreme 95
Avalokiteshvara, Buddha 15, 23, 31, 66
  manifestation of compassion 51

basis of imputation for I 57, 60-2, g
Behar spirits 12
Biwawa 75, 78-80
blessing initiation 55, 97
blessings 6, 66, g
bliss and emptiness (see also uncontaminated bliss) 44
Bodh Gaya 28
bodhichitta 48, 50, 71, g
  conventional and ultimate 23
  generating 19
Bodhisattva path 84
Bodhisattva vows 27, 42, 50

Bodhisattvas 31, g
body mandala 89, 90, g
Brahma 28, g
Buddha 25, 48, 76, g
  signs and indications 26
  twenty-seven deeds 75
Buddhadharma (see also Dharma) 15, 27, 29
Buddha families 51, g
Buddhahood 14
Buddha Shakyamuni 4, 19, 28, 72, 89, g
Butön Rinchen Drub 75, 82-3

central channel 43, g
chakra (see also channel wheel) 23, 43, g
channel wheel g
clear appearance 62, 63-5, g
clear light 49, g
Clear Light of Bliss 49
close retreat 53-67, g
  necessary conditions 55
  of *Migtsema* 11, 16, 53, 66
  preliminary practices 56
  preparations 55-6
commitment being 36-7, g
compassion g
  great 71, g
  unobservable 32
completion stage 15, 84, g
concentration being g
conscientiousness 53
conventional truth 26, g
crown ornaments 47

Dakas 26
Dakinis 26, 79
Dalai Lama 86
  1st, Je Gendundrub 6, 11, 86
  2nd, Je Gendun Gyatso 86
  3rd, Sönam Gyatso 5, 86
  5th 86
dedication 28-9
degenerate times 27, g
Deity (see also mandala Deities;
  Yidam) g
  worldly 71-2
Deity yoga 50
delusions (see also ignorance)
  15, 28, 53, 67
demon (see also maras, four) g
desire realm 21, g
Dharma (see also Buddhadharma;
  Je Tsongkhapa, teachings) 15,
  71, 84
  books 36, 50
  teachings 35
Dharma Protector (see also
  Dorje Shugdän) 71-95
  functions 71-3
Dharmakaya 21, g
Dharmakirti 35, g
Dharmavajra 89
DHI, letter 5, 37, 43, 44, 65, 66
divine pride 60, 62-3, g
Dorje Sangpo 13
Dorje Shugdän 72-3
  different aspects 75
  five lineages 90, 91-2
  mandala Deities 89, 90, 91
  nature and function 89-94
  previous incarnations 75-87
  relying upon 73, 92-4, 95-7
  sadhana 56, 90, 95, 97
  symbolism of his form 91
  synthesis of Three Jewels
  94
Drepung Monastery 85, 86,
  93
Drombi Heruka 80

Dromtönpa 20
dualistic appearance 15, g
Duldzin Dragpa Gyaltsän 75,
  83-5

eight Fully Ordained Monks 92
emanation (see also Manjushri,
  Buddha) 4, 25, 72, 75-6, 83-4
Emanation Body g
  Supreme 72, g
Emanation Scripture 11, 13, 47, 89
Emanation Temple 82
empowerment 97, g
  of Dorje Shugdän 73, 97
emptiness, correct view of 48, g
Enjoyment Body g
enlightenment 25, 28
Essence of Manjushri 20
expounding Dharma, gesture of
  23

Field for Accumulating Merit
  19-25, 89, g
  inviting 19-22
five lineages 90, 91-2
Foe Destroyer g
Form Body 26, 65
fortunate aeon g
four fearlessnesses 22, g
four noble truths 34, g
four protections 22-3

Ganden doctrine 4
Ganden Lhagyäma 11, 12, 14, 45,
  56, 97
Ganden Monastery 4, 84, 85
Ganden Pure Land (see Tushita)
Gelug Tradition 4
Gelugpa 4, 73, 92
Gendun Gyatso, Je 86
Gendundrub, Je 6, 11, 86
generation stage 15, 84, g
generic image g
Geshe Jatse 9
Geshe Palden 11

great fault, the 48
Great Treasury of Merit 49, 90
Guhyasamaja Tantra 49
Guide to Dakini Land 49
Guide to the Bodhisattva's Way of Life 53
Guru Tsongkhapa 8, 22, 43-5, 65, 67, 90
in-front generation 66
self-generation 57-60, 62-3
Guru yoga of Segyu lineage 3, 14, 90
benefits 13-6
history and lineage 11-3
Gyältsabje (see also Je Tsongkhapa, Father and Sons) 19, 20, 21, 84-5
Gyara Tulku Rinpoche 93
Gyuchen Gendunpai 13
Gyuchen Tashipa 13
Gyumä Tantric College 11
Gyutö Tantric College 85

Heart Jewel sadhana 97
Heruka 90, g
Heruka Tantra 49, 78
Highest Yoga Tantra 49, 84, g
Hinayana 50, 78, g
HRIH, letter 65
HUM, letter 65
Hundreds of Deities of the Joyful Land (see also *Ganden Lhagyäma*) 11

ignorance 33, 48, g
illusory body 49, 86, g
Indra 28, g
Infinite Aeons 73, 97
inherent existence g

Jambudipa 20
Jampel Nyingpo 20
Je Tsongkhapa (see also Guru Tsongkhapa)
autobiography 27

body, speech, and mind 26, 50
Dharma activities 50-1
emanation of Avalokiteshvara 14, 22
emanation of Maitreya 4, 20
emanation of Manjushri 3, 4, 14, 19, 22
emanation of Vajrapani 14, 22
Father and Sons 6, 19, 21, 33, 36, 43
qualities 4-5
teachings 47-8, 50-1
writings 50-1
Je Tsongkhapa's doctrine 14, 15, 23, 28
jenang 55
Jetsün Dragpa Gyaltsän 81
Joyful Land (see also Tushita) 21
Joyful Path of Good Fortune 29, 49, 65

Kadam Emanation Scripture (see *Emanation Scripture*)
Kadampa Tradition 20
Kalarupa 72, 90, g
Kalindewi 72
Kangyur 82, g
karma 62, 72
Kashyapa, Buddha 29
Khädrub Sangye Gyatso 13
Khädrubje (see also Je Tsongkhapa, Father and Sons) 19, 20, 21, 89
King of the Dharma 25, 56, 67
Kumbum Monastery 5
Kyabje Trijang Dorjechang 13, 73, 97

Lama Chöpa 89
Lama Losang Tubwang Dorjechang 89
body mandala 89, 90
Lamp for the Path to Enlightenment 48
Lamrim (see also stages of the path) g

Land of the Thirty-three Heavens 20
Land Without Combat 21
liberation 28, 48, g
lineage (see also Guru yoga of Segyu lineage) g
close 13, 15, 89
Lojong (see also training the mind) g
Losang Chökyi Gyältsän 72, 86, 89
Losang Dragpa 31, 89, g

Madhyamika-Prasangika 23, g
Mahakala 72, g
Mahamudra, Vajrayana 15, 49, 89, g
preliminary practice 89-90
union of great bliss and emptiness 44
Mahasiddha 80, g
Mahayana 50, 71, 78, g
Maitreya, Buddha 4, 11, 20, 21, 23, 45, g
mandala Deities 89, 90, 91
mandala offering 29, g
Manjushri, Buddha 11, 23, 31, 36-7, 47, 66, 82, g
disciple of Buddha 77-8
emanations 4, 15, 72, 75, 83
manifestation of wisdom 51
mantra 65-6, 67, g
of Manjushri 37, 65
maras, four 23, 65, 92, g
Meaningful to Behold 65
meditation break 44-5, 67
meditative equipoise g
gesture of 23
Meeting of Father and Son Sutra 76
Menkhangpa 15
merit 14, 25, 26, g
collection of 25, 26, g
Migtsema prayer (see also close retreat, of Migtsema) 12, 14, 31, 36, 45, 51-2

benefits 15
ritual healing practices 12, 15-6
Milarepa 76
mindfulness 53
miracle powers 4, 5, 82-3
of Biwawa 79-80
Mönlam Chenmo 85
moral discipline 22, 49-50, 91, g
Morchen Dorjechang Kunga Lhundrup 72-3
Mount Meru 20, g

Nalanda Monastery 78, g
Namkha Drime 20
Narthang Monastery 11
negative actions (see non-virtuous actions)
Ngamring Jampaling Monastery 11
Ngatrul Dragpa Gyaltsän 86-7
nine Great Mothers 92
non-virtuous actions 27, g
Nyungnä Lama 8

obstacles, pacifying 26, 33, 71, 91, 95
outer, inner, and secret 15
obstructions to liberation 65, g
obstructions to omniscience 26, 65, g
Ocean of Nectar 49
Offering to the Spiritual Guide 89, g
offerings (see also mandala offering) 27, 29, 55-6, 66
torma g
tsog g
ordinary appearance 15, 62, g
ordinary conception 15, g
Ornament for Clear Realization 75

Palden Sangpo 11-3, 14
Palden Yeshe 15

Panchen Lama
   1st, Chökyi Gyaltsän 72, 86, 89
   3rd, Palden Yeshe 15
Panchen Sönam Dragpa 75, 85-6
path (see spiritual path)
perfection of moral discipline 22
perfection of wisdom 22
Perfection of Wisdom Sutra 14, 49, 75, g
   in Eight Thousand Lines 23
Phabongkhapa, Je 13, 90
Phadampa Sangye 76
Pratimoksha g
   vows 27, 41, 49
Prayer of the Stages of the Path 41-2
preliminary practices
   for *Migtsema* retreat 56
   for Vajrayana Mahamudra 89-90
profound path 51, g
prostrations 26
protection circle 44
Protector, the great 4
puja g
Pure Land (see also Tushita) g
purification 14, 26, 27, 33, 65, 77
   by meditation on emptiness 57

rabnä puja 20
realizations 14, 26, 33
   of stages of the path 41-3
   of Sutra and Tantra 14
refuge, going for 19
rejoicing 27-8
Rendapa, Je 47
renunciation 48, g
requests, making 31-3
Reting Monastery 20
retreat (see also close retreat) 53
root Guru g
Root Tantra of Manjushri 3
Root Text of the Mahamudra, the Main Path of the Conquerors 89

Sachen Kunlo 91
sadhana (see also Dorje Shugdän, sadhana) g
Sakya Pandita 75, 80-2
Sakya tradition 73, 80
Samdrub Gyatso, Je 13
samsara 25, 48, 62, g
Sangha g
Secret Mantra (see also Tantra) 33, g
seed-letter (see also DHI; HRIH; HUM) g
Segyu lineage (see Guru yoga of Segyu lineage)
Segyu Tantric College 11
self-cherishing g
self-grasping 60-1, g
Sengei Ngaro, Buddha 4
Sera Monastery 85
seven limbs 25-9
seven types of wisdom 34-6
   receiving attainments of 36-41
Shakyamuni, Buddha (see Buddha Shakyamuni)
Shargangrima 6
Sherab Senge, Je 11
sickness and disease 5, 15, 26
six perfections (see also perfection of moral discipline; perfection of wisdom) g
Sönam Gyatso 5, 86
Song of the Eastern Snow Mountain 6
Spiritual Guide (see also root Guru) 25, 36, 72
   relying upon 84
spiritual path 5, 36
stages of the path 15, 41-3, g
   commentaries 49
   pre-eminent attributes 48
Stainless Space 20
statues of Je Tsongkhapa 6
Superior being g
superior seeing 48, g
Sutra g

Sutra for Eliminating Ajatashatru's Regret 77
Sutra Revealing the Abode of Manjushri 77
Symphony Delighting an Ocean of Conquerors 73

Tagpo Kelsang Khädrub Rinpoche 73, 75, 76, 97
Tagtsang Lotsawa 50
Tängyur 82, g
Tantra (see also Secret Mantra) 49
Tantric vows 27
Tashilhunpo Monastery 11, 82
Tathagata Lamp of the Nagas 77
ten directions g
ten Wrathful Deities 92
thirty-two major signs 26, g
three recognitions 67
training the mind 15, 49, g
tranquil abiding 48, 65, g
transference of consciousness 45, g
Treasury of Abhidharma 81
true cessation g
true origin g
true path g
true suffering g
Tsöndrupa 13
Tushita 4, 20-1, 63, 67
how to be reborn in 45

ultimate truth 26, g
uncontaminated bliss 26, 27, g
union of great bliss and emptiness 44, 50
Union of No More Learning 14, 23, 49, g
union that needs learning 49, g
Universal Compassion 49

vajra body, speech, and mind 51-2, g
vajra posture 63, g
Vajradaka burning offering 66, g
Vajradhara, Buddha 42, 49, 84, 89, g
Vajrapani, Buddha 15, 23, 31, 44, 66, 84, g
manifestation of power 19, 51
Vajrayana 42, 44, 50, 51, g
Vajrayogini, Buddha 78-9, g
vast path 51, g
Vasubandhu 81
Vinaya 84
Vinaya Sutras 49, 77, g
Vinaya vows 79
Virtuous Tradition 4
vows (see also Bodhisattva vows; Pratimoksha vows; Vinaya vows) 27, g

Wheel of Dharma 28, g
gesture of turning 21, 23
wisdom 14, 34-41, 71, g
collection of 25, 26, g
exalted 27, g
perfection of 22
wisdom being 36-7, g
Wisdom Buddha (see also Manjushri, Buddha) 4
wisdom swords 39
Wishfulfilling Jewel 97
wrong views 76

Yamantaka, Buddha 12, 90, g
opponent of obstacles 14-5
Yidam 90, g
Yiga Chödzin Palace 21, 63
Yöntän Zhirgyurma 41

Further Reading

JOYFUL PATH OF GOOD FORTUNE
The Complete Guide to the Buddhist Path to Enlightenment

Joyful Path of Good Fortune presents the complete Buddhist path to enlightenment in a form that is easy to understand and put into practice. Enriched with stories and illuminating analogies, it presents the essential meaning of all Buddha's teachings in the order in which they are to be practised, giving step-by-step guidance on all the meditations leading to full enlightenment. By following the instructions given in this book we can transform our life, fulfil our true potential, and discover for ourself and others a limitless capacity for peace and happiness.

"Geshe Kelsang Gyatso both delights in and has a profound insight into the entire range of the teachings of the Buddha. Difficult technical points are rendered into pleasantly readable prose, and the text as a whole is both absorbing and illuminating." – *Tibet Review*

640 pages, glossary, biblio., index.
Hardback £17.95/$29.95. Paperback £14.95/$24.95.

GREAT TREASURY OF MERIT
The Practice of Relying upon a Spiritual Guide

Great Treasury of Merit is a comprehensive explanation of *Offering to the Spiritual Guide* (Tib. *Lama Chöpa*), one of the most profound meditation practices of Mahayana Buddhism. In this highly acclaimed guide, Geshe Kelsang shows clearly how to rely upon a Spiritual Guide, the foundation of all spiritual attainments. He explains the three essential components of Buddha's Sutras and Tantras – the two preliminary practices of the stages of the path and training the mind; and the actual swift path to full enlightenment, Vajrayana Mahamudra. For those wishing to integrate all their spiritual practices into the Tantric swift path to full enlightenment, this book is a great wealth of spiritual guidance and an indispensable resource.

384 pages, glossary, biblio., index.
Hardback £15.95/$29.95. Paperback £13.95/$23.95.